To Glen

Hope you find this valuable —

Dr F. Kaslow

The Family Life of Psychotherapists: Clinical Implications

THE *JOURNAL OF PSYCHOTHERAPY & THE FAMILY* SERIES:

- *Computers and Family Therapy*
- *Divorce Therapy*
- *Family Therapy Education and Supervision*
- *Marriage and Family Enrichment*
- *Treating Incest: A Multiple Systems Perspective*
- *Depression in the Family*
- *The Use of Self in Therapy*
- *The Family Life of Psychotherapists: Clinical Implications*
- *Chronic Disorders and the Family*
- *Women, Feminism, and Family Therapy*

The Family Life of Psychotherapists: Clinical Implications

Florence W. Kaslow
Editor

The Haworth Press
New York • London

The Family Life of Psychotherapists: Clinical Implications has also been published as *Journal of Psychotherapy & the Family*, Volume 3, Number 2, Summer 1987.

The Haworth Press, Inc., 12 West 32 Street, New York, NY 10001
EUROSPAN/Haworth, 3 Henrietta Street, London WC2E 8LU England

Library of Congress Cataloging-in-Publication Data

The Family life of psychotherapists.

"Has also been published as Journal of psychotherapy & the family, volume 3, number 2, summer 1987" – T.p. verso.

Includes bibliographies.

1. Psychotherapists – Family relationships. 2. Psychotherapy. 3. Family psychotherapy. I. Kaslow, Florence Whiteman. [DNLM: 1. Family. 2. Psychotherapy. W1 J0859C v.3 no.2 / WM 420 F198]
RC454.4.F35 1987 616.89'14023 87-25107
ISBN 0-86656-683-X

Dedication

To my family of procreation, Solis, Nadine and Howard, who have intuitively known my desire to live fully in two worlds – the personal and the professional – keeping them somewhat apart yet definitely interwoven.

Florence W. Kaslow

The Family Life of Psychotherapists: Clinical Implications

Journal of Psychotherapy & the Family
Volume 3, Number 2

CONTENTS

The Family Life of Psychotherapists: Clinical Implications

EDITORIAL NOTE

The *Journal of Psychotherapy & the Family* is especially proud to publish this special issue focusing on the family life of psychotherapists. The *Journal* is dedicated to improving the arts and sciences of psychotherapy practice by focusing on the family and its role in the prevention, development and maintenance of psychopathology. The aim of the *Journal* is to provide the most well-written, accurate, authoritative, and relevant information on critical issues in the practice of psychotherapy with families. This issue, consistent with the *Journal*'s aim, intends to promote new insight into the complex interface between the work of psychotherapy and the work of family membership.

When we are called upon to treat fellow psychotherapists presenting with a family-related problem or when we ourselves know we need these services, we face an extraordinary set of challenges. These challenges are associated with the transposition of our personal family life with our objective and task-oriented work life.

This is a very important issue to me. When I founded the *Journal* in 1984 this was one of the topics I felt should be addressed as soon as possible. Why? Perhaps more than other professionals, psychotherapists, particularly those who frequently work with *family clients*, find difficulty in making the transition from work to their own family life and back again. Added to this, the recent discoveries of substance abuse and impairment among health care professionals, whose home life most certainly affects and is affected by their substance use, makes this issue of critical importance to all of us.

The divorce rate among psychotherapists is higher than the national average and one of the highest of any profession. Also, psychotherapists frequently spend so much of their energy tending to the problems of others that they devote little time to their own dilemmas and those that emerge within their family system. Moreover, though they are trained to recognize and evaluate the problems they see in their clients, often they are unable to see those emerging within their personal and interpersonal lives: they are too close to them.

Finally, psychotherapists frequently take themselves too seriously. They are unable to be separate, at least at home, from their profession and frequently and without being aware of it, treat family members and friend as clients.

The popular television program, "The Bob Newhart Show," though far from realistic, did illustrate the constant interrelationship between one's professional responsibilities and identities and one's marital and family roles. And though often humorous, our mixing of home and professional duties are stressful and, at times, difficult to manage.

Most psychotherapists would like to believe that they are aware of the significant mutual influences of work and family life. Few, however, have reported efforts to carefully assess the wanted and unwanted results of these influences and taken systematic measures to make improvements.

Perhaps more than any other profession, practicing psychotherapists who read this issue may wish to share this collection with another: spouse, children, or parent or some other family member or friend. It should help them understand us, themselves in relation to us, and the interpersonal relationships of psychotherapists.

This collection is the second issue of *Journal of Psychotherapy & the Family* to focus on personal issues. The last issue focused on the use of self in therapy, co-edited by Michele Baldwin and Virginia Satir. It sensitized the clinician to her or his own conscious and unconscious.

When I first decided the *Journal* needed such a special issue, Dr. Florence Kaslow was the first person who came to mind. She had recently completed an important edited volume, *Psychotherapy for Psychotherapists* (NY: Haworth, 1985). She is extremely knowledgeable about psychotherapists' families, and has one of the largest professional networks of any colleague I know. She has considerable experience in the editing role. She is former Editor of the *Journal of Marital and Family Therapy*, author/editor of 9 books, including *Psychotherapy for Psychotherapists*, which includes several chapters devoted to the family life of clinicians and co-author of *Dynamics of Divorce: A Life Cycle Perspective*. She was named Psychologist of the

Year in 1986 by Division 43 (Family Psychology) of the American Psychological Association and became President of the Division in 1987. Currently she is an adjunct professor of psychology in psychiatry at Florida Institute of Technology, and is Director of the Florida Couples and Family Institute (West Palm Beach) where she practices and supervises family therapy.

This edited collection is a compliment to Dr. Kaslow's familiarity with the influence on the field of psychotherapy. No other collection has included so many key individuals knowledgeable about the family life of psychotherapists.

Enjoy your reading and then pass it on.

Charles R. Figley, PhD
Editor

Introduction

Psychotherapy is a many splendored, multihued and complex tapestry that interweaves science and art, theory and intuition, cognitive processes and interventive skills. It occurs within many contexts including the larger socioeconomic, political and moral ones of the society in which it is conducted. Another important context is the personal world of the particular therapist – his or her family of origin and family of procreation or immediate universe of significant others and how these have shaped and continue to influence his or her personality, attitudes, behaviors, interpersonal skills, and values. For all of these, plus the sum total of the therapist's personal life experiences impact upon his or her workaday world as a teacher, supervisor or practitioner of psychotherapy in general, and family therapy specifically, since this is the main focus of this volume.

All of the contributing authors have attempted to analyze and synthesize their knowledge of the ongoing and reciprocal impact of the therapist's personal and professional worlds – the two-way flow between what one brings to and takes from being a member of one's own family to being a therapist or trainer of therapists who deal with it by treating, coaching or consulting others' families. A great deal of personal soul searching has gone into the creative process of generating these articles. In each instance, the exploration of one's personal journey and experience has been tempered by sound, rational, cognitive reflection and analysis.

Thus, each article reflects, as it must, the particular author's/authors' own style of *being in* his or her *personal* and *professional* world. Authors such as Paul, Coleman and Kaplan, and Philpot have permitted us some glimpses of their own private pathways into professionalism – the struggling and juggling of the myriad complexities and often covert and overt conflicts that mark the life of women who want and need to encompass the roles of wife, mother and therapist simultaneously in their lives. The reactions of husbands and children are important and influential, for we love them and treasure them. But, it is not the totality of existence – for women, anymore than it is for men.

And, female therapists' families, like those of male therapists, get stirred up and resentful when "Mom" or "Dad" seems to invest more time and energy in the families she/he sees at the office than in the one awaiting her/his involvement and caring at home. This is succinctly depicted in the articles by Kaslow and Schulman, and Coleman and Kaplan.

Guerin and Hubbard, and Winter and Aponte venture forth from a base line of exploring the family of origin of their trainees as this impacts positively upon or negatively impedes their ability to work with treatment families. They knowingly and sensitively traverse the unresolved and critical attachment and loyalty themes that underlie their trainee's interventions— making respectable once again the imperative that transference and countertransference issues must be raised to conscious awareness *and* worked through and that such training does not occur quickly. It is a long and continuous journey, worth the effort when seasoned therapists with a clear sense of how to use themselves effectively in treatment and training evolve from and through the process. Case vignettes illuminate their thinking and methodology.

In a highly theoretical paper, Catherall and Pinsof expand upon the work they've been doing in recent years on the ability to establish and maintain viable therapeutic alliances. They also predicate their work on a family of origin model and present different levels of alliance with the family as a system and its members as individuals who sometimes have conflicting goals. Further, they provide guidelines for therapists who wish to assess the quality of their alliances.

Piercy and Wetchler take the reader to another realm when they describe a didactic experiential workshop for facilitating the understanding of "the family work interfaces of psychotherapists" complete with elucidation of workshop activities.

Each of the authors cites the relevant literature which provides, taken as a composite across articles, a fine bibliography of the material available on the personal life of the therapist as it affects his or her professional self and therapeutic work. We have found writing these articles a provocative, stimulating and sometimes distressing experience and hope that reading them may provide a similar, if less intense, experience for you.

Florence W. Kaslow, PhD
Guest Editor

Reflections of a Therapist/Wife of a Therapist/Husband

Betty Byfield Paul

SUMMARY. The author shares some of her experiences of changing from a more traditional role of housewife and mother to a mode of combining career with marriage and motherhood. The emphasis here lies on the subtle changes that took place in her professional and personal relationship with her therapist/husband who entered the family therapy field before she did. The author has talked with more than a dozen therapist/wives and therapist/husbands to learn from the larger community what their experiences have been. This process of growth and development among therapist/wives and therapist/husbands is vital and important and is bound to impact their daily work with clients and organizations.

CONTEXT

When I first presented the substance of this article to Florence Kaslow, the editor of this volume, it was in outline form and was autobiographical in nature. At Florence's suggestion, I sought out and reflected with "other therapist/wives" in order to make my "reflections" more generic.

These therapist/wives, who are also friends and colleagues, responded most enthusiastically. Therapist/husbands volunteered also. I had no refusals. Almost everyone wanted their name mentioned. Several participants remarked that "these thoughts represent the top of a smoldering volcano."

Each telephone call or personal interview was made informally. I started out by asking the interviewee "to reflect with me" about being

---

Betty Byfield Paul, LICSW, a graduate of Bryn Mawr College and Simmons School of Social Work, is an Approved Supervisor of AAMFT. She has been on the faculty of the Arlington Public Schools, the New England Center for the study of the Family and Wheelock College, Center for Parenting Studies. She is currently in private practice in Lexington, MA. Mrs. Paul is a charter member of the American Family Therapy Association and is a fellow of the American Orthopsychiatric Association. She may be contacted at 26 Barberry Road, Lexington, MA 02173.

a therapist/wife of a therapist/husband or a therapist/husband of a therapist/wife. In each case, information streamed forth. The data seemed to be poised on the tip of each person's tongue. What was most surprising was that these colleagues shared so many experiences in common. General themes unfolded and gave structure to the paper. A lot of affect was shared in each interview.

I decided to intersperse my colleagues' reflections among mine so that the general themes could become clear to the reader. My uniqueness was not diminished in the process. On the contrary, I felt more and more energized as the paper developed. In the end, it became clear that these brave individuals and couples are still, in process, struggling to achieve inner peace and growth while surviving in a tumultuous, rapidly changing outer world.

> Countless psychological studies have shown that woman is still perceived by both men and women as Adam's rib – despite all the efforts of feminists from Lucy Stone to Simone de Beauvior. That is, she is defined not in terms of herself, but in terms of her relationship to men, Adam's rib, Adam's wife and mother of his children.
>
> *McClelland, 1965*

> Here we are again – women reflecting about themselves and men.
>
> *Therapist/wife #1, 1986*

> I don't understand the frame! What do you mean "Therapist/wife of a Therapist/husband"? I don't like the word "*of*". I won't accept that frame. It should be the therapist wife *and* the therapist husband.
>
> *Therapist/wife #6*

Certain external events sometimes have a more profound effect on our lives than we can possibly imagine. For me, such an event was the Women's Movement, an expression of society's questioning about woman's place. The Movement made it possible for Simmons School of Social Work to expand its formerly full-time program to include a pilot part-time program for women with vital family responsibilities.

As an educated woman (Bryn Mawr, 1947), I had begun to get restless and itchy intellectually six months after our first child was born, but there had been no part-time career-directed educational opportunities open to me at that time. I had applied to Simmons' full-time program in 1953, but changed my mind when the female director asked me what I would do if the "baby ran into a fire burning in the fireplace." My family's needs came first. I did not have the wherewithal to hire full-time domestic assistance, nor did I really want such help.

So in the early 1960s, when Simmons opened a part-time program, I was delighted and energized. I felt that I could both organize and take appropriate care of my husband, daughter, son and house while pursuing the study of social work on the side. Actually, at that time I wasn't sure it was social work that I wanted; it was the profession that had become available through its new flexible program policy. It represented to me an ethical ticket into the outside world. Being a practicing therapist was totally beyond my ken at that time. I wanted something to balance what for me was an overly-domesticated life.

Before 1963, my primary goal in life had been to be a "good wife and mother." Like some other women who are now in the therapist/wife category:

> It was very important to me to be a "significant mother." It never occurred to me to work full time.
>
> *Therapist/wife #2*

Being a "good wife and good mother"—that was the role that the women in my family had played on both my mother and my father's side of the family through the generations. This was a role emulated in other families, too!

> My mother felt that putting a Mrs. in front of your name was more important than putting a PhD after it.
>
> *Therapist/wife #3*

In my world at that time, having both a Mrs. and a PhD did not seem possible. My mother and grandmother were the only models of married femininity that I had experienced. Partially, it was a role I admired; partially, I felt that it was a passive cop-out. I had appreciated their "presence" and availability, yet felt that they didn't appear to be doing *anything*. What is "anything"? Looking back now (1986), I can see that I had "bought into" the ridiculous myth that "wifing" and "mothering" were equivalent to doing nothing.

Before my marriage in 1950, I had had a superb job on the New York Times as a facilitator for the New York Times Youth Forums. This meant that I moderated forums throughout the greater New York community and selected from those groups an adolescent for the weekly radio program with Dorothy Gordon. After my marriage and a move to the Middle West to "be with" my husband, who was a medical doctor with the Air Force, I somehow lost my emotional and intellectual drive towards a career. Job-wise, I was then more than satisfied to be a secretary to an Air Force General. After marriage, I made no effort to seek a position similar to the one I had had on the New York Times in Dayton, Ohio, where Norman and I lived for a year and a half.

Once I became a mother in 1952, I was immediately drawn subtly and loyally toward old family patterns (Boszormenyi-Nagy & Spark, 1973) . Work outside the family for money was not an occupation that "our women" pursued. "The old tape" clicked in, and I became in my mind an auxiliary, or as my 85-year-old mother recently said when describing herself, "I always enjoyed being a back seat driver like my mother was." I did what my mother did and her mother did before her; I worked for no pay inside and outside the home (Paul & Paul, 1975). I did an enormous amount of volunteer work, yet there was no plaque given to me after serving for eight years. I received long since disposed of candlesticks. (I have always hankered after a plaque, because my husband has a long row of them.)

After that experience and four years of Freudian analysis (1959-1963), it became very clear that I should put my energy into a profession of my own. During this analysis, I began to be aware that I had needs of my own to fulfill, a thought that had not occurred to me before. In my case, I felt that I needed and wanted professional training *in addition* to fulfilling my roles as wife and mother.

When Simmons' part-time program opened up in 1963, my daughter, Marilyn, was ten and my son, David, was eight. They were in school until 3:00 p.m. My husband was becoming established in his chosen field among an array of radical innovators (Bernal & Ysern, 1986); we both thought that he could do without me as a sounding board or hostess.

Therefore, he and I, after considerable consultation with each other, promoted my getting deeply involved in Simmons' part-time program. Nevertheless, I became a "closet graduate student" (a closely-kept secret from my children and at times from myself). I made a rule never to bring my work home. I always was present "spic and span" when the children got home from school. I wanted to give the impression that I was "all theirs"; and I was.

Therapist/wife of therapist/husband #3 put it this way:

> My identity and self-esteem always depended more on my personal relationships than on my career. My husband's professional life impacts much more on our intimate space than mine does. I always gave my undivided attention to my family.

That is how it was for me, too, in those days.

Seemingly, my venture to social work school had total emotional and financial support of my therapist/husband. Before I started on the program, he invited me to work with him after I received my MSW. After all, his parents had worked together running an appliance store. They had been working collaborators in a "Mama & Papa" venture.

Despite the support, I remember the guilt I felt one night when I left husband, daughter and son eating TV dinners happily while I went off to study in the Lexington library for an exam. I spent several analytical sessions on my guilt until I was reminded that the supermarkets were filled with nutritious TV dinners. Not every woman was "at home" cooking over a hot stove. "I'm an ego man," said my analyst; "You could manage three children and a PhD if you wanted to."

Once I entered social work school, I became as fascinated as I had been at Bryn Mawr with the intellectual life. Courses in Human Development, Psychoanalytic Theory, Psychosomatic Illnesses and Casework and my first year placement at Boston Family Service kept me very busy and enlivened. My second year placement was at the Arlington Public Schools where I remained after I graduated. This choice of a job reflected the same personal needs I had had before graduate school. It was three-quarters time, and I was home when the children came home from school.

Leaving social work school with an MSW in 1966, I felt that I could not work with my psychiatrist husband as planned. I felt much less educated in the "family therapy field" and had no accepted experience in a territory in which he was now considered a "pioneer" and "expert." I did not want to appear publicly as Norman's "rib." (Occasionally, I still do. As late as 1984, a director of a well-known family institute "forgot" to put my name on a flyer when announcing a program that Norm and I were doing together.)

With the graduate degree in hand, I had the need to establish myself as a social worker separate from him. I wanted to strike out on my own, much to his and my surprise. (I was breaking rule #1, don't surprise your husband.)

In my interview with therapist wife #1, she remembers her similar reaction when she finished her PhD in psychology. The first thing that she recalled was how apprehensive she was about entering the field that her husband was already in.

> I had a BA in English and had decided to do my master's in psychology. Once I got my degree and we were both PhDs, it became very important to me to be seen as separate.
>
> *Therapist/wife #1*

Six years after I graduated from Simmons, the Multiple Family Group became the vehicle through which Norman and I began to work two and one-half hours a week together.

> On Thursday night each week, four to eight families converged in the library/studio to learn from each other, to teach each other, and to teach us the leaders.
>
> *Paul and Paul, 1985*

My evolving role as a leader of that group could best be put into four stages: that of (1) apprentice; (2) beginning family therapist; (3) intermediate family therapist; and (4) valued collaborator. This developmental process took approximately 14 years.

The apprentice stage was marked by a true mixture of admiration and dismay as I became exposed to what I thought of as Norm's radical and brilliant interventions on the one hand and his total male chauvinism on the other. This "apprenticeship stage" was also experienced by other therapist/wives I interviewed here who chose to work closely with their husbands.

> It was an incredible mixed blessing . . . I felt like an apprentice (1971) . . . I felt just fascinated. I loved the process and admired him enormously. Yet, I wondered whether I could do any of this therapy away from his auspices. During the apprentice state, I never felt competitive.
>
> *Therapist/wife #6*

The first year Norm's patience or benevolence was remarkable as one male after another dropped out of the group. Used to his "cuddling," they were scared off by what they thought of as my hostility, because I treated them as equal to the women. Norman treated the men more gently and seemed to recognize that beneath their bland distancing appearance, there was much brittle anxiety. My goal had been impartiality. The male members of the group felt threatened by my too direct inquiries about their vulnerabilities. In general, however, I followed Norm's lead and viewed myself basically as a student.

The next two stages brought many more conflicts between us. These were stages at which I began to have a few opinions of my own. Other wives in the process of becoming therapists report similar experiences.

> I began to be aware of a difference in style . . . I began to have ideas . . . he seemed surprised.
>
> *Therapist/wife #4*

During stage three (intermediate family therapy), the issue of working together as true co-leaders began to become apparent.

> I wasn't aware of the number of intimate things we hadn't talked about together until they were brought up in the couples group we did together.
>
> *Therapist/husband #2*

Not wishing to relinquish working together, by 1975 I asked to be a true co-leader. Co-leading the Multiple Family Group in this final stage made it necessary for us to learn to communicate clearly and intimately both professionally and personally. Fees are now shared equally.

Neither of us was prepared for this kind of partnership. Realizing we hadn't had an equal professional partnership through the work in the Multiple Family Group challenged us to work towards that goal. Neither Norm nor I had experienced or seen true co-leadership or partnership modelled in a married couple. In 1986, we are friends, lovers; we work together; we work separately; yet, still today we are continuing to work on just what partnership in the '80s means to us.

> It was a shock . . . I was like a wall. . . . It took awhile . . . the unexpected sparring . . . neither of us were prepared for partnership.
>
> *Therapist/husband Norman Paul*

We have discovered that old habits die very hard and slowly. Last week, I bought a special portable radio for my own use. This week, Norm took it to the Family Process Board Meeting in Lisbon (1986) without asking to borrow it. The image of Adam's rib came up again; I was furious.

Missing some of the old comforts of the way things were, we are presently writing a new book along with a colleague. The name of it is "The Joy of No Change."

AFTERTHOUGHTS

It becomes apparent that the need to be Adam's rib and for Adam to have a rib is a most complicated pnenomenon. Some invisible elements contributing to this are: (1) the seductive aspects of being fused into one entity; (2) the inability to experience the benefits of being alone; and (3) the terror of having to work out the details of a true dialogue. True dialogue may lead to gender empathy, an elusive ingredient in the world today.

The study of marriages and of each partner simultaneously includes a need to consider reciprocating identifications and when they interfere with a sense of self, or when they lead to ready integration of the other into self. When smothering appears, how is this handled? And all of this is influenced by the invisible shadows of families of origin, models for behavior often faded by time. World events, wars and movements likewise exert their impact, stirring thought and behavior often disconnected from their sources.

So what is our profession's family secret? If these reflections represent "the tip of a smoldering volcano," what lies underneath? Now in their fifties and sixties, the therapists interviewed here are still struggling for answers. The heat remains on us to find them, because in our daily work we set ourselves up as "experts," "professionals" in the art of living. We coach others in how to play the game of life, and we get paid to do so.

If we cannot work out our own issues of power and intimacy, can we be of any help to clients or to the community-at-large?

It occurred to me that we are therapist/wives, therapist/husbands and therapist/couples in search of role models. In our field do we have couples who can be couple/mentors? I was once asked who was my female mentor in the field. "Virginia Satir," I answered. But Virginia has no spouse. Who is my husband's mentor? Murray Bowen, but LeRoy Bowen is not a therapist.

So here we are late-life therapists in search of some models. So far there does not seem to be any. It takes a lot of courage to know how to mentor yourself.

ACKNOWLEDGEMENT

Reflecting with me on this project have been my colleague, Nicholas Clark, LICSW and therapist/wives and therapist/husbands: Milo Benningfield, PhD, Anna Beth Benningfield, PhD; Bunny Duhl, EdD, Meredith Kantor, EdM, Laura Chasin, LICSW, Jeanette Kramer, Chuck Kramer, MD and Judith Grunebaum, LICSW; Faye Snider, LICSW, and my therapist/husband, Norman L. Paul, MD. Thanks are also expressed to my bi-monthly support group, Therapeutic Resources of Brookline, MA for editorial assistance.

REFERENCES

Bernal, G. & Ysern, E. (1986). Family therapy and ideology. *Journal of Marital and Family Therapy*, *12*(2), 129.

Boszormeny-Nagy, I. & Spark, G. M. (1973). *Invisible loyalties: reciprocity in intergenerational family therapy.* New York: Harper and Row. Reprinted NY: Brunner/Mazel, 1985.

McClelland, D. C. (1964). Wanted: A new self-image for women. In R. J. Lifton (Ed.) *The woman in america* (p. 73). Beacon Press.

Paul, B. B. & Paul, N. L. (1985). Outpatient multiple family group. In Mirkin & Koman (Eds.) *Handbook of adolescents and family therapy.* New York: Gardner Press.

Paul, N. L. & Paul, B. B. (1975). *A marital puzzle: Transgenerational analysis in marriage counseling*. New York: W. W. Norton.

Family-Work Interfaces of Psychotherapists

Fred P. Piercy
Joseph L. Wetchler

SUMMARY. This paper provides an overview of the literature related to family-work interfaces for psychotherapists. An outline of a didactic experiential workshop is presented as one way to help the practicing therapist explore these interfaces. The workshop examines: (a) how the therapist's family of origin may affect his/her work, (b) how a therapist's present marriage/family may affect his/her work, (c) how a therapist's work may affect him/her personally (and indirectly his/her family), and (d) how a therapist's work may affect his/her marital/family life.

I. A SUMMARY OF THE LITERATURE

Psychotherapists are in a unique profession that exposes them to a multitude of joys and sorrows. Each day can be an emotional roller-coaster with its ebb and flow of human experience. Throughout this process, psychotherapists are expected by their clients to be many things – comforter, sage, seer, and soothsayer. They must exhibit wisdom and equanimity in the face of turmoil. Their work is far from routine.

What about the family lives of psychotherapists? How does their work affect their own lives and those of their families? How do their families of origin affect their choice of a profession and their day-to-day work? Further, what happens to their work when they experience marital or family problems themselves? To date there are few answers to such questions.

Fred P. Piercy, PhD, is Associate Professor and Director of Training and Research, Family Therapy Doctoral Program, Department of Child Development and Family Studies, Purdue University, West Lafayette, IN 47906. Joseph L. Wetchler, MS, is a doctoral student within the Family Therapy Doctoral Program, Department of Child Development and Family Studies, Purdue University.

The Effect of Providing Psychotherapy on the Psychotherapist

Psychotherapy is indeed a difficult profession. Some call it "impossible" (Greenson, 1966). Therapists often spend long hours listening to their clients' problems, and many make personal sacrifices to their work. This may lead to burnout, an emotional and physical exhaustion which stems from overwork and a high degree of emotional involvement. Burnout is prevalent among mental health professionals (Edelwich & Brodsky, 1980; Freudenberger, 1974; Maslach, 1978), and can lead to a lack of concern for one's clients (Maslach, 1976) and even feelings of anger toward them (Farber & Heifetz, 1982). Furthermore, burned-out therapists may experience psychosomatic symptoms and increased family conflicts (Farber & Heifetz, 1982).

Many authors have suggested sources of stress inherent in the field of psychotherapy (English, 1976; Freudenberger, 1974, 1975, 1985; Greben, 1975; Greenson, 1966; Kubie, 1971; Maslach, 1978; Schlict, 1968; Wheelis, 1958, 1966; Whitfield, 1980). Generally, these writers believe sources of stress stem from societal and personal expectations as well as personal isolation, overwork, and difficult client loads. Freudenberger and Robbins (1979) and Friedman (1985) suggest that therapists should take steps to combat these problems by avoiding becoming overly responsible for their clients' problems, taking time away from work, and replenishing their thoughts through outside training.

An increasing number of researchers have examined the problem of burnout and stress in the mental health field (Bermak, 1977; Cherniss, 1980; Cherniss & Egnatios, 1978; Daniels, 1974; Edelwich & Brodsky, 1976; Farber, 1983; Maslach, 1976, 1978; Pines, Aronson & Kafry, 1980; Pines & Maslach, 1978). Farber and Heifetz (1982) found that therapists attributed the occurrence of burnout to nonreciprocated attentiveness and giving, the difficulty of dealing with patient problems, and discouragement due to the slow and erratic process of therapy. The most stressful client behaviors appear to be suicidal statements, patient anger toward the therapist, and severe depression (Deutsch, 1984; Farber & Heifetz, 1981).

Chessick (1978) and Fine (1980) hypothesize that the continuous bombardment with client problems and the tendency to remain isolated can lead to depression. This has received some empirical verification as Deutsch (1985) found that 57% of the therapists she surveyed had experienced depression in their lives and over one-fourth of her sample has been in therapy for depression. Studies of suicides among psychiatrists (Freeman, 1967; Rich & Pitts, 1980) and psychologists (Mausner & Steppacher, 1973) provide further cause for concern.

The Family-Work Interface

How do stresses such as those mentioned above interact with the family life of the psychotherapist? After all, the psychotherapist does not live in a vacuum.

The affect of the therapist's family (past and present) on his/her work. Transgenerational family therapists (e.g., Bowen, 1978; Framo, 1975; Kerr, 1981; Kramer, 1985) suggest that therapists' personal issues stemming from their families-of-origin may block their ability to solve certain therapy problems. These authors believe that to be an effective therapist one must first work on resolving issues in his/her own family of origin. There even has been speculation that certain life experiences in one's family-of-origin may lead to the choice of a profession in the mental health field (Gurman, Kniskern, Jacobson & McGoldrick, 1985; Henry, Sims & Spray, 1971, 1973). In their classic survey of psychotherapists, Henry et al. (1973) reported no evidence of any uniqueness among psychotherapists that could be attributed to their choice of profession. However, they did notice an early trend toward intellectual pursuits of psychotherapists in childhood. These findings must be viewed with caution because of the lack of comparable data on the family lives of members of other professions.

Several authors suggest that psychotherapists may be attracted to the field due to a need for "controlled intimacy" at their clients' expense (Bernstein, Wacks & Christ, 1969; Bugental, 1964; Dreyfus, 1967; Guggenbuhl-Craig, 1971; Hammer, 1972; Henry, 1966; Sharof & Levinson, 1964). Others have expressed concern that therapists may attempt to fulfill intimacy needs that are lacking in their present families through their clients (Framo, 1975; Zweben & Deitch, 1976). It seems probable that life stresses in a therapist's own family may affect his/her work (Cray & Cray, 1977; Flaherty, 1979; Givelber & Simon, 1981; Nadelson, Notman, Arons & Feldman, 1974). Research in this area has been scant and the results are mixed. Waldroop and Hurst (1982) found that therapists did not appear to gratify their neurotic needs through working with clients and that the majority of this sample had rewarding home lives. Greenspan and Kulish (1985) found that therapists' life stresses did not affect premature termination in long-term psychotherapy, although Farber and Heifetz (1982) report that stresses at home lead to transient feelings of burnout in psychotherapists.

The affect of the therapist's work on his/her family. A few authors have discussed the impact of being a psychotherapist on the therapist's own family (Charny, 1982; Freudenberger & Robbins, 1979; Warkentin, 1963). This may be due to psychotherapy's traditional focus on the individual; or perhaps, as Henry et al. (1973) discovered, therapists have concerns about disclosing their personal family issues.

Psychotherapists generally agree that they are often too tired to hear their families' problems and are frequently unable to switch back to being a family member after a day at the office (Charny, 1982; Freudenberger & Robbins, 1979; Kaslow, 1984a). Further, there may be a clash between one's clients and one's own family regarding personal commitment and issues of intimacy; such comparisons between clients and family may present problems (Warkentin, 1963).

The research in this area has revealed some interesting findings. Farber and Heifetz (1982) report that 75% of their sample of therapists cited having problems with work issues spilling over into their family lives. Farber (1983) found that therapists are concerned with overanalyzing problems at home, allowing their psychological-mindedness to inhibit their spontaneity in social situations, and treating their spouses as clients.

Deutsch (1985) found that 82% of the therapists she surveyed reported having experienced relationship difficulties and that 47% had sought therapy for relationship problems. Many therapists discussed having relationship conflicts with their spouses and children. Those who belonged to "two clinician" families often reported overanalyzing their own dynamics.

In a survey of psychiatric residents examining the interaction of training and interpersonal relationships, Taintor, Morphy, Seidan and Val (1983) found that 62% of their sample reported increased sensitivity and awareness to others, 33% reported increased personal problems, 54% found their marriage to be helpful in the training, 12% felt their marriage hindered their training, and 12% were separated or divorced during this period. Several respondents perceived distancing from their spouses that resulted from the training experience.

For some therapists, complications arise when they try to get therapy for their family problems. Spouses are often hesitant to enter therapy with their therapist/spouse for fear of being sided against by the two helping professionals (Deutsch, 1985; Kaslow, 1984a). Some therapists report being unable to enter therapy because of their difficulty in finding a therapist with whom they are not personally or professionally involved (Deutsch, 1985). Further, it may be difficult to find a therapist with the special skills necessary to treat this unique population (Kaslow, 1984b).

Summary of Our Own Research

Our own research (Wetchler & Piercy, 1986) focused upon the stressors and enhancers of marital and family life for family therapists. The subjects were 110 members of the Indiana Association for Marriage and Family Therapy who responded to a state-wide membership survey (a 43% response rate). They were asked to identify and rank order various marital/family stressors and enhancers that they believed emanated from their work as family therapists.

The analyses of these stressors and enhancers provided a wealth of data. Perhaps the most noteworthy and optimistic finding was that respondents checked significantly more ($t = 16.6, 109, p < .001$) enhancers than stressors. In fact, more than twice as many enhancers ($X = 7.7$) were checked than stressors ($X = 2.8$).

The enhancers most frequently checked included "Acceptance of own part in marital/family problems," "Development of communication skills," and "Greater appreciation of own marital/family strengths." The item with the highest mean ranking was "Greater ability to prevent potential family problems."

The stressors checked most frequently and ranked most stressful were "Little time left for own marriage/family" and "Little energy left for own marriage/family."

Stressors and enhancers also were examined in terms of respondents' (a) gender, (b) work setting, (c) theoretical orientation, (d) number of hours worked, (e) income, (f) age, and (g) marital status. Our results seem to suggest that monetary success in family therapy may represent a double-edged sword. Family therapists making over $30,000, for example, were more likely to find it difficult to listen to their own spouses/families than those making less than $30,000. Similarly, those therapists conducting over 25 hours of therapy per week were more likely than those working less than 25 hours to look for marriage and family problems where none existed.

While our study represents a first step in examining empirically this important subject, much more needs to be known. On a practical level, we must begin to look for ways to harness the growth-enhancing features of the work-family interface and prevent or diminish concomitant risks. The remainder of this paper describes one means of addressing this formidable task.

II. A DIDACTIC-EXPERIENTIAL WORKSHOP

A therapist's work and family life continually affect one another in mutually interactive, reciprocal ways, as reflected in Figure 1. While accepting the systemic nature of these work-family interfaces, we have found it helpful to focus our workshops on various two-part components of these ongoing cycles. These components include (a) how a therapist's family of origin may affect his/her work, (b) how a therapist's present marriage/family may affect his/her work, (c) how a ther-

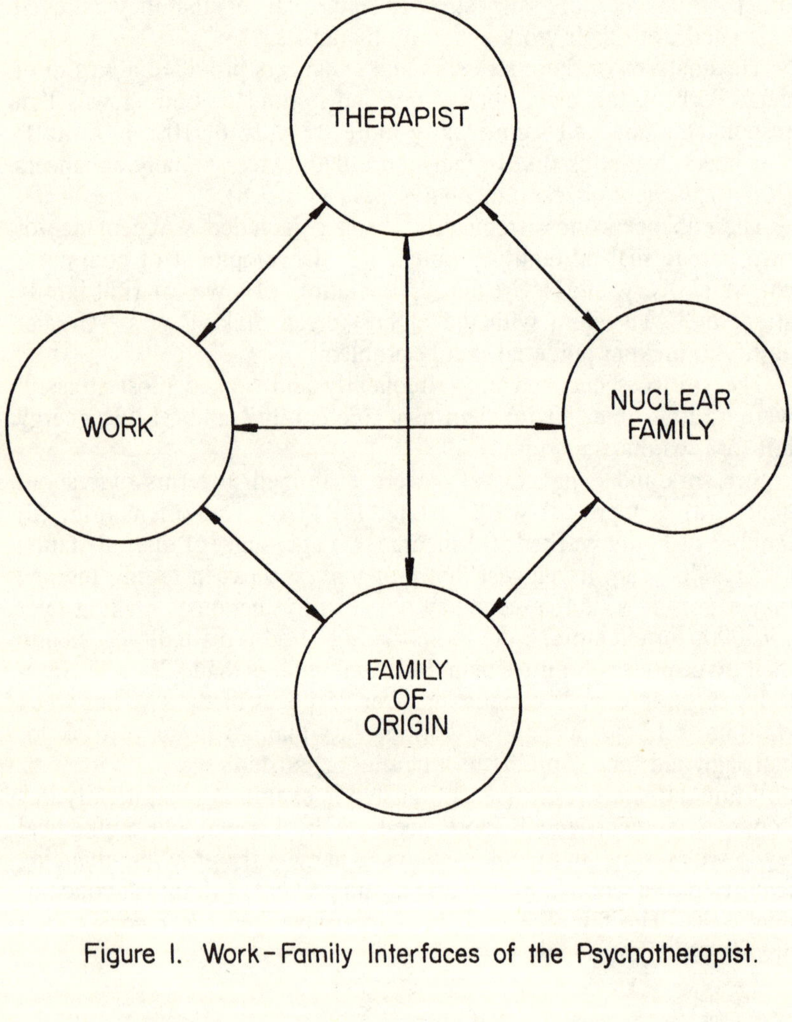

Figure I. Work–Family Interfaces of the Psychotherapist.

apist's work may affect him/her personally (and indirectly his/her family), and (d) how a therapist's work may affect his/her marital/family life. Each of these components is discussed briefly below, along with possible activities for the exploration of each component. The information is presented informally, as if directed toward workshop participants, to aid in its adaptation to that context.

How a Therapist's Family of Origin May Affect His/Her Work

Let's discuss how the family you grew up in affects your work. Since all of you have a family history, it is not surprising that you will frequently make connections between your family of origin and the clients you see. Framo (1968), for example, states:

> As I treated more and more families I have become used to reliving each stage of my own family life cycle during sessions, in a series of flashbacks at once compelling and fearsome, fascinating and despairing, growth promoting and regressive. While I am conducting treatment sessions with my surface calm and importance, hiding behind my degrees and the trappings of my profession, evaluating the dynamics of the family before me, figuring out the strategy, avoiding the traps, I communicate to the family only a small portion of the emotional connections I make with them, the places where we touch. (p. 19)

Such connections will regularly be made. They are part and parcel of your relatedness to your past. These connections can even relate to the type of therapist one chooses to be – a warm Rogerian, an efficient behaviorist, an enterprising private practitioner. It is no accident, for example, that Albert Ellis, who overcame a sickly childhood in New York developed an active (many non-New Yorkers would say aggressive!) kind of pull-yourself-up-by-your-bootstraps therapy. Nor is it surprising that Carl Rogers, who grew up in a religious family and attended Union Theological Seminary, developed a therapy with theological and humanistic underpinnings. Similarly, Neil Jacobson, a leader in behavioral marital therapy, found his place as a child by being a rebel. It made sense that when he entered a psychoanalytically-oriented graduate program that he would rebel and become a behaviorist (Gurman, Kniskern, Jacobson & McGoldrick, 1985). Indeed, our roots run deep.

Gurman (1985) was only half kidding when he said:

> Structural therapists are those who need to be in control of other people; behavioral therapists are those who require order and certainty; strategic therapists are those who fear their own impotence, and therefore require a team to let them do what they already think is right; and psychodynamic therapists, of course, are those who were either born Jewish or believe they should have been!

Kramer (1985) identifies typical statements made by her trainees about how their family-of-origin experiences affect their conduct as therapists. For example:

> I'm a middle child, a go-between, and I find myself defending and talking for individuals.
>
> I'm not sure about my role when I work with families where the anger is up front. My anxiety level rises and I want to put a cap on it, just as I did as a kid.
>
> I don't know what it's like to live with siblings since I never had brothers and sisters. It's also hard for me to treat mothers of young children; maybe that's too close to my own situation. (p. 159)

Your past makes you what you are today and cannot be left at home in the morning.

Workshop Activities

1. *Roles From Family of Origin*. Each workshop participant is given a sheet of paper with the following questions on it (adapted from Janine Roberts, personal communications, 1985). After writing one's answers the participant will share his/her answers with another person. A large group discussion follows regarding ways to prevent *family-of-origin messages* from negatively affecting one's work.

a. What roles did you have in your family of origin?
b. What topics could not be discussed?
c. How were disagreements handled?
d. What emotion was rarely expressed in your family of origin?
e. If you were to write a book about living in your family of origin, what would you title it?
f. What themes and/or roles from your family of origin (as identi-

fied by the previous questions) are present in your therapy sessions and/or your family life today?

2. *Videotaped Interface Examples*. When family interface workshops are scheduled on a weekly basis it is possible to ask participants to bring in videotapes of difficult current therapy sessions. Therapists are asked to consider how their own family-of-origin issues may have inhibited their therapeutic effectiveness. They pre-cue the videotape to where they got "stuck," and discuss the issues from their own family-of-origin that "hooked" them. These tapes, and the discussions that emanate from them, can provide enlightening learning experiences for all (Keller & Protinsky, 1985).

How the Therapist's Present Marriage/Family Affects His/Her Work

Therapists often bring their current life struggles to their therapy sessions. This may create difficulties when treatment families present problems that are similar to the therapist's unresolved issues (Kramer, 1985). The intensity of feelings associated with shared problems may "hook" a therapist who is unable to maintain a certain degree of objectivity. For example, if you just had an intense argument with your own spouse you may be unable to empathize with an opposite sexed client engaged in a similar struggle. Likewise, if you are currently angry at your own child's school performance you may be unduly critical of a treatment child with a similar school problem.

Specific family life cycle events may affect your work. Events such as getting married (Flaherty, 1979), becoming pregnant (Nadelson, Notman, Arons & Feldman, 1974), and the death of a family member (Givelber & Simon, 1981) may distract you from your clients.

Some therapists facing severe family crises, such as the loss of a loved one, may try to escape by becoming immersed in their work. This can become a real problem if these therapists unconsciously designate one of their clients to replace their lost loved one (Givelber & Simon, 1981). Framo (1975) states that therapists are more likely to try to meet their needs through their clients' families when these needs are not being met at home. Such dependence on clients can interfere with treatment. Consequently, it is important to inspect your own interface issues to discover if you may be misdirecting your own search for need fulfillment.

On the positive side, your nuclear family can enhance your work. The experiences that you have in your own family can both provide important "on-the-job training" and serve to broaden your perspectives on life. It certainly adds a greater depth to therapy when you can personally relate to your clients' problems. Further, individuals and families are more likely to trust you when they feel that you understand them and have "walked in their shoes."

Workshop Activities

The following sets of questions should be considered silently for several minutes, then discussed, one-at-a-time in small groups.

1. What are the presenting problems of clients you are currently "stuck" with in treatment? Are their problems similar to ones you are currently experiencing, or have experienced in the recent past? How can you separate your clients' issues from your own?
2. What is your stage in the family life cycle? What life cycle event are you currently facing? How are you dealing with it? Has your way of responding to your clients changed as a result of your situation? How has your situation affected your clients? How can you prevent this event from interfering with your work?
3. How might your work be meeting needs (like love or respect) that could or should be met at home? Is there anything wrong with this? Explain.
4. How have your marital and family experiences made you a *better* psychotherapist?
5. What marital/family presenting problems should you *not* treat? That is, which issues are "too close to home"?

How a Therapist's Work Affects Him/Her Personally

Providing psychotherapy can be personally stressful in a variety of ways. The suicide rate among helping professionals gives one emphatic indication of this stress. Physicians in general are more prone to suicide than people in other professions (Ross, 1973; Steppacher & Mausner, 1974). Psychiatrists are most at risk; they kill themselves at a rate twice as great as what would be expected (Rich & Pitts, 1980). During a recent five-year period 30 psychiatrists killed themselves, compared, for example, to seven gynecologists and no thoracic surgeons. There also appears to be a trend toward high suicide rates among psychiatric residents (Craig & Pitts, 1968; Russell, Pasnau & Taintor, 1975). Female psychologists have been found to be *three* times more likely than the general population to kill themselves (Mausner & Steppacher, 1973). The high suicide rate for female psychologists may well be due to role strain, the stress to excel both as a wife and as a professional (Mausner & Steppacher, 1973). These results on female psychologist suicide are consistent with results found by Deutsch (1984) that female therapists report greater work-related stress than males do.

There are many other plausible explanations for high suicide rates among therapists—stress and long hours, the anguish seen day after day, perfectionism, or the possibility that one may enter a helping profession to be healed (Rich & Pitts, 1980). Or perhaps the professionalism many therapists are taught to project keeps them from claiming their own humanity and handling the tragedy that is part of their work. This raises several important questions for you to discuss in the next workshop activity.

Workshop Activity

Have small groups discuss the following questions/issues in this order:

1. Why do you think there seems to be more suicides among helping professionals? What implications does your answer have for your own practice?
2. Does tragedy toughen you or chip away at you? Is it a true professional who learns to take distance and cut off (Framo, 1975)?
3. How can family members support you in stressful times?
4. What steps can you take personally to reduce the stress of your work? Which of these steps are you willing to commit yourselves to in this group?

After each group member has discussed the above questions and committed him- or herself to an action plan to reduce stress, instruct each to write the plan on a 3″ × 5″ card, put it in an envelope, and write his/her name and address on the envelope. Explain that six months from today you will mail each group member the personal "commitment" back. Each person may then evaluate his/her success in actualizing the commitment. (This written commitment often increases one's motivation to follow through.)

How a Therapist's Work May Affect His/Her Marital and Family Life

Your work as a therapist may affect your marital/family life both positively and negatively. As an example of a positive, we *really* appreciate our wives after conducting therapy sessions with certain couples in "cat-and-dog" marriages. Some of our difficult clients can make us appreciate what is good about our own families.

However, being a therapist can also negatively impact on family life. Below is a composite case example which illustrates some of the risks to our own marital and family lives mentioned by Charny (1982), Kaslow (1984a) and others, that may be inherent in our work.

> Dave was a bright, articulate, hard working, slightly compulsive individual who received his PhD about 15 years ago. During his doctoral work, Dave met and married Judy. He was attracted to her soft-spoken manner, noncompetitiveness, dependency on him and the interest she demonstrated in his work and life dreams. She made him feel important. She was also interested in having a family, and before long two beautiful baby girls were on the scene. Dave wanted to be a real partner in parenting, but he also wanted to do well in his work, and he found that it was difficult to do both. It made sense that Judy take on most of the parenting chores while he provided a secure future for his family. And one has to work *hard* to provide such a future (particularly if you are just a little bit compulsive).
>
> Dave was gone several nights a week, and when he arrived home he had little energy or interest in hearing the frustrations of Judy's day. He needed time away from the family to decompress and relax. Judy also needed time away, and quite a few arguments arose because of the "insensitiveness" each one saw in the other. When Dave went to conferences and weekend workshops, Judy felt overwhelmed and complained of being abandoned. The dependency Dave found initially so attractive in Judy became a rock around his neck. The drudgery and dullness of home life stood in sharp contrast to the increasing excitement of Dave's work.
>
> Dave's consultations and speaking engagements were beginning to increase. He was developing a fine reputation as a therapist. His clients were making him feel important and necessary. At the same time, Judy's wide-eyedness and adoration began to fade. When he walked in the door, Dave was faced with dirty diapers and a tired, increasingly disgusted wife.
>
> As the years passed, the babies grew up, but Dave's relationship with Judy continued to erode. He was growing professionally, his self-confidence was never higher, but Judy's life as mother and homemaker did not seem to change. Dave felt like he had been developing and she had not.

Dave had become something of an expert on families, and his own family did not measure up to his yardstick of what family life should be. Some of the individuals, couples, and families he saw in therapy were growing and were demonstrating the intimacy, warmth, and fairness that he yearned for in his own family.

When he would bring his expectations up to Judy, she seemed to use his profession against him. She knew his weak spots, and learned to strike with deadly accuracy. One of her favorite comebacks was, "And you call yourself a therapist." She really knew how to hurt! And as the kids got older, they also learned how to zap him. For example, he valued open communication, yet they would be withdrawn and secretive. In a hundred ways, they could kick the throne out from under dear old dad.

Sometimes Dave thought that, because of his training in family dynamics and human behavior, his own expectations were too high. Being a perfectionist seemed to be adaptive in graduate school, but it made him miserable as a husband and father.

Years passed and Dave developed quite a following in his community, was looked up to in his professional association, and became more and more active professionally. With such professional adulation, Dave found it harder and harder to return home to the mundane demands of his wife and children.

Judy eventually divorced Dave and took custody of the children. In the silence of his new apartment, Dave sometimes wondered, if I had become a plumber, would I still be married?

Our response to Dave is that plumbers get divorced, too. Yet Dave's case brings to light ways your work may carry with it potential risks or stressors to your marriage/family life.

Workshop Activities

1. Put each of these questions on a blackboard or overhead transparency and have small groups discuss them: What are your reactions to Dave's experience? With what stressors can you identify? Would the stressors be different for female therapists? How? In what ways can you prevent some of the stressors Dave experienced?
2. Have each workshop participant complete the questionnaire on stressors and enhancers of marriage/family life used in our previous study (Wetchler & Piercy, 1986). Then share with the large

group the general results of that study so they can compare our results with their own ratings.

3. Have the large group brainstorm strategies for lessening some of the more severe stressors identified in the questionnaire activity above. (You may also wish to have the group members write their action plans down so they also may be returned in six months.)

CONCLUSION

Very little attention has been given to the family life of the psychotherapist. The present article has attempted to survey relevant literature on this subject and present workshop ideas aimed at helping the practicing therapist examine the reciprocal effects of work and family in his/her own life. The workshop is intended to be adapted to various groups and leadership styles. It is *not* a cookbook.

As nurturers of other's lives, psychotherapists must not neglect their own. The present article is offered as one way to support this proposition.

REFERENCES

Bermak, G. (1977). Do psychiatrists have special emotional problems? *American Journal of Psychoanalysis*, *37*, 141-146.

Bernstein, S., Wacks, J. & Christ, J. (1969). The effect of group psychotherapy on the psychotherapist. *American Journal of Psychotherapy*, *23*, 271-282.

Bowen, M. (1978). *Family therapy in clinical practice*. New York: Aronson.

Bugental, J. F. T. (1964). The person who is the psychotherapist. *Journal of Consulting and Clinical Psychology*, *28*, 272-277.

Charny, I. W. (1982). The personal and family mental health of family therapists. In F. W. Kaslow (Ed.), *The international book of family therapy* (pp. 41-53). New York: Brunner/Mazel.

Cherniss, C. (1980). *Professional burnout in human service organizations*. New York: Praeger.

Cherniss, C. & Egnatios, E. (1978). Is there job satisfaction in community mental health? *Community Mental Health*, *14*, 309-318.

Chessick, R. D. (1978). The sad soul of the psychiatrist. *Bulletin of the Menninger Clinic*, *42*, 1-9.

Craig, A. G. & Pitts, F. N. (1968). Suicide by physicians. *Diseases of the Nervous System*, *29*, 763-772.

Cray, C. & Cray, M. (1977). Stressers and rewards within the psychiatrist's family. *American Journal of Psychoanalysis*, *37*, 337-341.

Daniels, A. K. (1974). What troubles the trouble-shooters? In P. Roman & H. Trice (Eds.), *The sociology of psychotherapy* (pp. 191-214). New York: Jason Aronson.

Deutsch, C. (1984). Self-reported sources of stress among psychotherapists. *Professional Psychology: Research and Practice*, *15*, 833-845.

Deutsch, C. (1985). A survey of therapists' personal problems and treatment. *Professional Psychology: Research and Practice*, *16*, 305-315.

Dreyfus, E. A. (1967). The search for intimacy. *Adolescence*, *2*, 25-40.

Edelwich, J. & Brodsky, A. (1980). *Burn-out: Stages of disillusionment in the helping profession*. New York: Jason Aronson.

English, O. (1976). The emotional stress of psychotherapeutic practice. *Journal of the American Academy of Psychoanalysis*, *4*, 191-201.

Farber, B. A. (1983). The effects of psychotherapeutic practice upon psychotherapists. *Psychotherapy: Theory, Research and Practice*, *20*, 174-182.

Farber, B. A. & Heifetz, L. J. (1981). The satisfactions and stresses of psychotherapeutic work: A factor analytic study. *Professional Psychology*, *12*, 621-630.

Farber, B. A. & Heifetz, L. J. (1982). The process and dimensions of burnout in psychotherapists. *Professional Psychology*, *13*, 293-301.

Fine, H. J. (1980). Despair and depletion in the therapist. *Psychotherapy: Theory, Research, and Practice*, *17*, 392-395.

Flaherty, J. A. (1979). Self disclosure in therapy: Marriage of the therapist. *American Journal of Psychotherapy*, *33*, 442-452.

Framo, J. (1968). My families, my family. *Voices: Art and Science of Psychotherapy*, *4*, 18-27.

Framo, J. (1975). Personal reflections of a family therapist. *Journal of Marriage and Family Counseling*, *1*, 15-28.

Freeman, W. (1967). Psychiatrists who kill themselves: A study in suicide. *American Journal of Psychiatry*, *124*, 846-847.

Friedman, R. (1985). Making family therapy easier for the therapist: Burnout prevention. *Family Process*, *24*, 549-553.

Freudenberger, H. J. (1974). Staff burnout. *Journal of Social Issues*, *30*, 159-164.

Freudenberger, H. J. (1975). The staff burn-out syndrome in alternative institutions. *Psychotherapy: Theory, Research and Practice*, *12*, 73-82.

Freudenberger, H. J. & Robbins, A. (1979). The hazards of being a psychoanalyst. *The Psychoanalytic Review*, *66*, 275-296.

Givelber, J. & Simon, B. (1981). A death in the life of therapist and its impact on the therapy. *Psychiatry*, *44*, 141-149.

Greben, S. E. (1975). Some difficulties and satisfactions inherent in the practice of psychoanalysis. *International Journal of Psychoanalysis*, *56*, 427-434.

Greenson, R. (1966). That "impossible" profession. *Journal of American Psychoanalytic Association*, *14*, 9-27.

Greenspan, M. & Kulish, N. M. (1985). Factors in premature termination in long-term psychotherapy. *Psychotherapy*, *22*, 75-82.

Guggenbuhl-Craig, A. (1971). *Power in the helping profession*. New York: Spring.

Gurman, A. (1985). Research in family therapy. Presentation given at Purdue University, West Lafayette, IN.

Gurman, A. S., Kniskern, D. P., Jacobson, N. S. & McGoldrick, M. (1985). Choosing a theoretical orientation in family therapy. Paper presented at the American Association for Marriage and Family Therapy Conference, New York.

Hammer, M. (1972). *The theory and practice of psychotherapy with specific disorders*. Springfield, IL: Charles C. Thomas.

Henry, W. E. (1966). Some observations on the lives of healers. *Human Development*, *9*, 47-56.

Henry, W., Sims, J. & Spray, S. (1971). *The fifth profession*. San Francisco: Jossey-Bass.

Henry, A., Sims, J. & Spray, S. L. (1973). *Public and private lives of psychotherapists*. San Francisco: Jossey-Bass.

Kaslow, F. W. (1984a). Treatment of marital and family therapists. In F. W. Kaslow (Ed.), *Psychotherapy with psychotherapists* (pp. 79-100). New York: Haworth.

Kaslow, F. W. (Ed.) (1984b). *Psychotherapy with psychotherapists*. New York: Haworth.

Keller, J. & Protinsky, H. (1985). Family therapy supervision: An integrative model. In F. P. Piercy (Ed.), *Family therapy education and supervision*. New York: Haworth.

Kerr, M. E. (1981). Family systems theory and therapy. In A. S. Gurman & D. P. Kniskern (Eds.), *Handbook of family therapy* (pp. 226-264). New York: Brunner/Mazel.
Kramer, J. R. (1985). *Family interfaces: Transgenerational patterns*. New York: Brunner/Mazel.
Kubie, C. S. (1971). The retreat from patients. *Archives of General Psychiatry*, *24*, 98-106.
Maslach, C. (1976). Burned-out. *Human Behavior*, *5*, 16-22.
Maslach, C. (1978). The client role in staff burnout. *Journal of Social Issues*, *34*(4), 111-124.
Mausner, J. & Steppacher, R. (1973). Suicide in professionals: A study of male and female psychologists. *American Journal of Epidemiology*, *98*, 436-445.
McGoldrick, M. (1982). Through the looking glass: Supervision of a trainee "triggers" family. In R. Whiffen & J. Byng-Hall (Eds.), *Family therapy supervision: Recent developments in practice*. London: Academic Press.
Nadelson, C., Notman, N., Arons, E. & Feldman, J. (1974). The pregnant therapist. *American Journal of Psychiatry*, *131*, 1107-1111.
Pines, A., Aronson, E. & Kafry, D. (1980). *Burnout: From tedium to* personal growth. New York: Free Press.
Pines, A. & Maslach, C. (1978). Characteristics of staff burnout in mental health settings. *Hospital and Community Psychiatry*, *29*, 233-237.
Rich, C. L. & Pitts, F. N. (1980). Suicide by psychiatrists: A study of medical specialists among 18,730 consecutive physician deaths during a five-year period, 1967-1972. *Journal of Clinical Psychiatry*, *41*, 261-263.
Ross, M. (1973). Suicide among physicians: A psychological study. *Diseases of the Nervous System*, *34*, 145-150.
Russell, A. J., Pasnau, R. O. & Taintor, Z. C. (1975). Emotional problems of residents in psychiatry. *American Journal of Psychiatry*, *132*, 263-267.
Schlict, W. J. (1968). The anxieties of the psychotherapist. *Mental Hygiene*, *52*, 439-444.
Sharof, M. R. & Levinson, O. (1964). The quest for omnipotence in professional training. *Psychiatry*, *27*, 135-149.
Steppacher, R. C. & Mausner, J. S. (1974). Suicide in male and female physicians. *Journal of the American Medical Association*, *228*, 323-328.
Taintor, Z., Morphy, M., Seidan, A. & Val, E. (1983). Psychiatric residency training: Relationships and value development. *American Journal of Psychiatry*, *14*, 778-780.
Waldroop, J. A. & Hurst, J. C. (1982). The psychotherapist and one-way intimacy. *Psychotherapy: Theory, research and practice*, *19*, 48-53.
Warkentin, J. (1963). The therapist's significant other. *Annals of Psychotherapy*, *4*(1), 54-59.
Wetchler, J. L. & Piercy F. P. (in press). The martial/family life of the family therapist: Stressors and enhancers. *American Journal of Family Therapy*.
Wheelis, A. (1958). *The quest for identity*. New York: Norton.
Wheelis, A. (1966). *The illusional man*. New York: Norton.
Whitfield, M. (1980). Emotional stresses on the psychotherapist. *Canadian Journal of Psychiatry*, *25*, 292-296.
Zweben, J. E. & Deitch, D. A. (1976). The emergence of primadonnahood in prominent psychotherapists. *Voices*, *12*, 75-81.

When Mother Is a Family Therapist (The Impact of Being a Family Therapist on One's Family of Origin and Family of Creation)

Carol L. Philpot

SUMMARY. The author explores the impact her profession as a family therapist has had on her family of origin and creation. In addition to her personal reflections on her experience as wife/mother/therapist over the past decade, she also shares the commentary of family members. Her observations strike a balance between the special stresses placed on herself and her family due to her profession and the advantages her skills provide in dealing with family life. She concludes with a reminder that therapists too are human and should accept themselves as such.

I sit here on the pool deck between my bikini-clad nineteen-year-old daughter and my twenty-two year old son's equally nude girlfriend, listening to reggae on their ghetto blaster, trying to "catch some rays," and ponder the impact of being a family therapist on my family of creation. Inside the house my sixteen-year-old son giggles loudly at his own ludicrous jokes, basking in the attention of two friends who have spent the night after their weekly dungeons and dragons game. My oldest son is "revving up" his recently purchased treasure, a twelve-year-old MGB with no brakes, but with an oil leak and rust holes in the hood, while his friends stand around in awe, discussing the next step in what appears to be a perpetual repair job. The basketball floats in the pool where it was left (or blown by the wind, depending upon which account you prefer to believe) after the vigorous game earlier in the day. My husband is seeing patients at his office in his sweaty tennis togs, having gone there directly from our Sunday morn-

---

Carol L. Philpot, PsyD, is Associate Professor of Psychology at Florida Institute of Technology, Melbourne, FL, and Licensed Psychologist and Licensed Marriage and Family Therapist in private practice in Indian Harbour Beach, FL.

ing tennis match with our best friends. And it occurs to me, that the answers, at least several of them, surround me at this very moment. Knowing the dangers of disengagement and enmeshment (Minuchin, 1981, 1984) and prizing the ultimate goal of differentiation (Bowen, 1976, 1978, 1981), I have helped to create this multifaceted family, this lovable monster which pulsates through the walls of our two-story home and escapes into the yard outside.

An interesting twist, this questions I have been asked to address. A reviews of the literature produces numerous articles on the impact one's family or origin and creation has on one's career choice (Racusin, Abramowitz & Winter, 1981) and therapeutic effectiveness (Seeman, Weitz & Abramowitz, 1976; Feld, 1982; Harvey, 1980; McGill, 1983), but little has been written which explores the mirror image of that relationship. Exactly what is the effect of being a family therapist on one's *own family*?

In a chapter investigating the personal and family mental health of family therapists, Charny (1982) probes the negative side of this influence, describing the traps the therapist encounters in interacting with his loved ones at home. He is quick to point out that family therapists are not immune to the same sort of difficulties they treat every day in their offices; in fact, there is an extremely high rate of family breakdown among these professionals. He delineates eleven additional stresses accumulated as a function of the professional identity which amplify the expected familial conflict intrinsic in all human relationships (Charny, 1980). He concludes his chapter with the suggestion that family therapy trainees and their families undergo family therapy to prepare them to cope with the normal vicissitudes of life as well as the hazards of the profession.

In viewing family therapy as an essential component of the training process, he is joined by many others (for example, Guldner, 1978; Kaslow, 1982). However, there are special considerations to be managed in the event a family therapist or trainee opts for treatment (Kaslow, 1984). These issues range from his or her embarrassment and reluctance to self-disclose to attempts on his or her part to collude or compete with the therapist as co-expert. Thus, even in treatment, the professional status of the family therapist can be detrimental.

On the flip side of the chart, at the 9th Family Therapy Network Symposium, Dalton and Manning (1986) presented the results of their recent, as yet unpublished, study of the pros and cons of being a therapist on parenting one's own children. Respondents in their sample submitted opinions based on personal experience that struck a balance between the negative impact of too much analysis, over-responsibility, and extremely high expectations, and the more positive contributions of knowledge of developmental issues and acquisition of specific skills in communication and behavioral training.

On a more general level, we know that many family therapists have chosen this field of endeavor in order to work out their own problems with spouses, children, siblings or parents (Ferber, Mendelsohn & Napier, 1972), and that through an exploration of their family dynamics, they come to a better understanding of themselves as a part of a multigenerational system (Bowen, 1976, 1978, 1981; Guerin & Guerin, 1976). With that knowledge comes a greater tolerance for human weakness, forgiveness of past and present wrongs, acceptance of the necessity for conflict and fluidity in life and an awareness of and appreciation for the contradictory aspects of themselves. They learn how they contribute to the problems of other members of the family while recognizing each of them is caught up in a larger system, doing the best they can with the skills they have available at the time. Such growth can have a positive effect upon their families in spite of the dangers inherent in "knowing too much."

"ONE WOMAN'S STORY"

In the tradition of Freud (Freud, 1953) and Piaget (Ginsburg & Opper, 1969) I have chosen the time-honored single case study method in order to examine this question in greater depth. The case under the microscope is one with which I am intimately familiar – my own. Obviously some of the observations reported will be idiosyncratic, arising from my particular history and family situation. On the other hand, most will be generalizable. They support many of the conclusions drawn by Charny (1982) and Dalton and Manning (1986).

Some background information may be helpful in understanding the setting of this particular case. I am in my mid-forties, female, a mother of three children, two boys (age sixteen and twenty-two) and a girl (age nineteen), and have been married to a physician for twenty-six years. I have been a therapists for twelve years, the last six of which have been heavily focussed on family therapy. I live in a small town (population 30,000), teach in the graduate program of a local university, and have a private practice. My husband and I have always been active in the community and our names are individually and collectively highly recognizable (the big fish in a small pond syndrome). I was a high school English teacher before my children were born and a mother for nine years before I began my formal study in psychology – a fact which may alter my perspective on the influence being a therapist has on my mothering skills. Almost a decade of parenting had already taken place before I knew enough in the way of formal theories to either correct or botch the job I was doing based on my parents' example and common sense.

As is typical of my approach to such matters, when I began to collect data for this article, I immediately polled my family, requesting their input and perspective on the issue. The first response received was from my sixteen-year-old son whose quick come-back is characteristic of his attitude and reveals much about our interaction—"The effect of having a family therapist in our family is having to do *stupid* things like this!" Clearly he has no fear of disagreeing with me, nor of being critical of his parents (he is, after all, sixteen), and he is expressing the derogatory attitude toward the values of his mother, the therapist, that Charny (1982) cites. Fortunately for the purposes of this paper, other family members were more cooperative, so that the following remarks represent a collective effort, not merely the skewed impression of the therapist herself.

EFFECTS ON FAMILY OF ORIGIN

I was raised by an engineer father and "schoolteacher-become-housewife" mother who placed a high value on education and achievement, but who do not, to this day, put much stock in the profession of psychology. Both of them express pride in what they perceive as my educational achievement and in my thriving practice (because I must be helping people or they wouldn't keep coming to me), but have great concern for my physical health and possible neglect of my family of creation because I am overextended. They see my profession as giving my life some meaning (for some strange reason), especially since housework did not seem to satisfy me (also for some strange reason), and because of that they are happy for me. In spite of the fact that my father's ability to handle and motivate people as the president of his own firm was highly influential in my becoming interested in working with others, he sees "common sense" as having more value than all the psychological theories in the world. He views my interest in psychology as a stage which will dissipate when I get out of it what I need. (A smart man, perhaps.) My mother is concerned about burnout, afraid that listening to all those problems will only depress me as well. In general, when asked directly, my parents respond with tolerance and pride, but a vague hint of disrespect for my chosen profession.

Ironically, but not at all surprisingly, when family crises occur, I suddenly become the expert, whose consultation is sought and heard with new interest. Whether the topic is divorce, child-rearing, organizational development, or personal depression, my analysis and suggestions are generally accepted and found useful. Thus, though they consciously appear to be guarded and skeptical, unconsciously my parents appear to derive benefit from my training. My own explanation of this apparent contradiction is the difficulty we all have accepting the role reversal in which the child becomes the expert in human living.

Also of note were my father's enthusiastic contributions to the family genogram I put together as a student and my mother's subsequent interest in researching her own roots. Employing a Bowenian approach (Bowen, 1976, 1978, 1981; Framo, 1981; Guerin & Guerin, 1976), we were able to explore formerly delicate issues in the larger context of the extended family. Using genealogy as the label, we succeeded in gaining the distance necessary to reduce defensiveness and come to a better understanding of one another. And yet none of this was officially recognized as a contribution of psychology or family therapy, thus avoiding the stigma such nomenclature carries.

On the other hand, my younger brother (four and a half years my junior), also an engineer, lost his skepticism during the painful process of divorce and has openly accepted psychology and the skills I have acquired as useful and relevant. For him, his wife, his ex-wife, and her present husband, and all their respective progeny, I have become the unofficial family therapist. My skills in divorce mediation and marriage counseling, and my knowledge of the special problems of blended families and child development have been put to the test on a fairly regular basis for the past six or seven years. Additionally my brother has called upon me on numerous occasions to act as a consultant with regard to his business, seeing my experience in systems theory and group processes as valuable in motivating his employees and running his large engineering firm smoothly. Indeed my expertise in this area has, in many ways, increased our closeness and our areas of common ground.

An interesting phenomenon, characteristic of family and friends of therapists, as well as of other professionals, is their eagerness to seek free consultation for problems which do not seem major enough to them to warrant the financial investment and time commitment of "official treatment." Thus the therapist is put in the awkward position of knowing what needs to be done while recognizing the dangers and ethical dilemmas inherent in the dual role of attempting to treat family members. In my case, intervention has been limited to psycho-education and some minimal medication. Nevertheless, it is not unusual for family members to expect help and to react negatively if that help is refused, as though the therapist were withholding relief capriciously. Despite explanations regarding the complications of dual roles, they often continue to request "advice." For those of us who have entered the field of family therapy partially because we want to serve others, saying "no" to loved ones is particularly difficult. Remaining a therapeutic friend and not crossing that line into therapy is an ongoing battle.

Also on the negative side, the mistaken notion on my part that because I was the expert in human relations and should, therefore, "have it all together," prevented me, until recently, from turning to other family members in times of stress for support and understanding. Although my birth position as oldest child of two might dictate this response anyway (Dinkmeyer, 1979; Nichols, 1984), I feel my need to appear free of personal problems played a greater role in my reluctance to self-disclose. Difficulties in living which I accept in others as merely evidence of being human, I do not tolerate well in myself. Thus the support of extended family is not sought when indeed it could be helpful and I deprive myself of a valuable resource.

EFFECTS ON NUCLEAR FAMILY

Husband/Wife Dyad

On the plus side of being a family therapist, specific skills in conflict resolution, negotiation decision-making, communication and behavioral contracting prove very useful in the daily interaction with one's spouse. A basic acceptance of differences as evidence of individuality and differentiation, not rejection, a respect for the rights and values of others, and recognition that disagreement is an unavoidable part of daily living are all concepts which allow for a less stressful relationship. Awareness that change is inevitable and that people develop at different paces, allows for tolerance of temporary periods of emotional separation which might otherwise have resulted in dissolution of the marriage. Knowledge of life cycle stages (Carter & McGoldrick, 1980; Levinson, 1978) puts individual crises in the context of a life span and normalizes behavior change which might otherwise have been alarming. A conscious effort to identify how one contributes to marital strife and what changes can be implemented to bring about greater harmony is another benefit of training.

Nonetheless, a major complaint of my spouse is my tendency to be a therapist, analyzing and interpreting, rather than a wife who becomes emotionally involved and meets him on a person-to-person level. The philosophical and theoretical stance of the therapist-wife can put the nontherapist-husband in a one-down position which results in resentment and frustration.

Additionally, tremendous changes in my value system resulting from my training and experience as a therapist, have made me much more liberal, tolerant and desirous of intimacy and warmth than I once was. The growth has been confusing to my spouse. Perhaps, as Charny (1982) points out, I have become unrealistic in my expectations, demanding idealistic standards of marital interaction and unable to accept less than perfection. It is quite true that much of the emotional satisfaction I experience comes from work, where sessions are emotionally-charged, intimate, and genuine and result in greater satisfaction and happiness of the clients. The mundane trivialities of home-life are pale by comparison.

In my particular case, the loss of energy to deal with family life due to long, stressful workdays is doubled, since both my husband and I work in service-oriented professions, ministering to people in time of distress and need. We both come home with our emotional resources depleted and tend to withdraw into ourselves for a renewal of energy. Because my husband is as involved in patient care as I am, I do not have to deal with a spouse who is jealous of the time and attention I give to my clients. He understands. He is not home most of the time himself. Neither of us demands attention from the other; consequently time and strength to develop our own relationship is meager and the relationship suffers the results of neglect.

Added stress comes from the fact that both of us are in leadership positions in the community and therefore in the spotlight much of the time. I experience the need to present a "good marriage" to the public, to be a positive role model for my clients seeking marital therapy. The pressure, much like that placed on ministers, does not allow us to be an average couple with our areas of dissatisfaction and inadequacy like everyone else. This results in a public pseudo-mutuality which is hypocritical and personally distasteful.

Finally, exposure to the intimate details of many marriages provides me with a large comparison base for my own marriage. This has both negative and positive effects. Some marriages appear to work at a relatively low level in contrast to the ideal and that fact gives encouragement. As a therapist I find myself reflecting, "At least we're not that bad!" Conversely, an occasional couple will achieve, partially with my help, a level of intimacy and pleasure in one another that my husband and I seem unable to attain in our marriage. At those times, I question the value of continuing the struggle of the past quarter of a century. As Stuart (1980) would say, my marriage does not always meet the comparison level of alternatives.

Dissatisfactions notwithstanding, my overall evaluation is that the clinical skills and theoretical knowledge have done more to preserve our marriage than to undermine it.

Parent Dyad

As we all know, it is very important that the parental dyad be united and strong in a functional family system (Bowen, 1976, 1978, 1981; Minuchin, 1981; Satir, 1967; Vobel & Bell, 1981). Unfortunately, one effect of the therapist-spouse becoming the expert in child development and parenting techniques may be the abdication of that responsibility by the nontherapist-parent which causes an immediate power imbalance in the parental dyad. My husband feels a loss in terms of his competency as a parent, becoming ambivalent or dogmatic alternately about his position. Much of the time he leaves the parenting to me which results in a distancing from our children that he does not really want. His withdrawal from the role of parent is a double-edged sword – I not only have no one to consult regarding parental decisions, but in his eyes I am also fully responsible for the success or failure of those decisions. Thus, by deferring to my greater knowledge, my husband avoids accepting any blame for the difficulties our children experience. Much of this, assuredly, is my own "fault," since I openly exprcssed annoyance in the early years when my husband's behavior directly contradicted widely accepted principles of healthy family interaction. Rather than face continued criticism, he basically stopped parenting. In recent years we have worked at correcting this imbalance and are making progress toward that end. I suspect, however, that in families where one parent is trained in child-rearing principles and the other is not, the untrained spouse is often intimidated and weakened, which results in the very imbalance we, as therapists, seek to correct.

Effects on Parent/Child Subsystem

As Dalton and Manning (1986) point out, knowledge of both child and adult developmental issues, awareness of the interaction effect between parents and children, recognition of the triangle and the impact of marital dysfunction on child behavior are all helpful in working with our children. Systems theory makes us aware of the tendency to scapegoat our children and we can no longer view their problems in terms of their failure alone. In other words, as family therapists, we see the *system* as dysfunctional and do not present our children as identified patients. This adds an extra burden of responsibility, as we, unlike many parents, explore our own contribution to our children's difficulties rather than seeing them as bad kids deserving of punishment or in need of treatment. At the same time, a systemic approach provides insight and possible solutions to our children's problems in terms of a change in our own behavior. Certainly general communication skills, acceptance of a wide variety of human behavior as normal, use of specific behavioral techniques, tolerance and patience are beneficial in the demanding job of parenting. Empathy and understanding may also be increased in the therapist-parent/child relationship.

My children had relevant observations regarding their perception of having a therapist-parent which deserve attention here. They readily praised the open communication and the nonjudgmental, accepting atmosphere at home, which allowed them to share with me many areas of concern not generally shared with parents—sex, drugs, adolescent depression, and so on. They expressed appreciation that disagreement was not only allowed but encouraged, that philosophic differences were expected and respected and that empathy for others was highly valued. They were proud that their peers clustered at our home and seemed to envy them because their parents were so "cool." Indeed, I became, for many of my children's acquaintances, a "therapist-friend" in times of distress.

My children recognized that they were each valued for their own particular strengths and assets and were not expected to be like each other. They were each encouraged to pursue a variety of interests and their needs were met on an individual basis. I became for my two older children, a role model, of sorts. My twenty-two-year-old son has chosen psychology as a profession. He is, by nature, a philosopher, a sensitive and deep thinker who covers up his substance with a smooth, superficial exterior. He has always questioned established rules and values and has come to believe that psychology provides a legitimate and effective avenue to help bring about the changes he would like to see in the world.

My daughter has become a therapeutic confidante for many of her friends. She has been the super-achiever in the family, winning awards and scholarships on a state, national and international level for her scientific research. She is the child who has chosen a career in medicine, creating her own major in psychobiology as an undergraduate. (What better way to emulate both parents at once!) She long ago surpassed her mother in achievement, an objective she openly admits pursuing. Clearly she is not afraid of hard work or competition and her sights are set on goals which she might not have considered feasible had she not had the role model of a mother who is also a professional.

It remains to be seen what effect, if any, my profession will eventually have on my youngest son. Presently, he is, as Charny (1982) points out, in adolescent rebellion and "symbolically insulting" (1982, p. 49) both of his parents by being noncommunicative at home and academically underachieving at school. Having been through this with my oldest son, I call to mind my mother's favorite saying, "This too shall pass."

Which brings me back to an earlier remark regarding the influence of formal training on parenting skills. Although I often use what I have learned with my own children, it seems the skills are only a supplement to the basic philosophy of respect and trust with which I was raised. Had I not been so fortunate as to have the parents I did, perhaps I would suffer more from the confusion expressed by so many therapists in the Dalton and Manning (1986) study who were immobilized with their own children due to conflicting theories in the literature.

Among the negative aspects of having a therapist-parent, is the unnatural status of having a "too-tolerant, too-understanding" parent. Direct quotes from my children best convey this thought.

"It's nice that you are more understanding and tolerant than most parents but it's hard to rebel when you don't have much to rebel against."

"Trouble is you understand *too* much. It makes us positively paranoid. You know why we do and say what we do before *we* do."

A common trap of clinicians is that we psychologize too much—analyzing every occurrence and seeing underlying motives in every event. We tend to make "a big deal" out of situations that most parents would ignore and to understand and accept other situations that would produce major objections in nontherapist-parents. We fall into the psychologist role when it might be more productive to be just a parent.

Closely related is our inability to see family problems in simplistic terms. Awareness of cyclical interactions, developmental stages, underlying motivations, and competing theories of intervention make quick, effective responses difficult. And as my daughter pointed out, if I change my theoretical conceptualization in midstream and thus alter my behavioral tactics, my response is confusing to the children.

As is true for the husband/wife dyad, parenting takes emotional energy and patience which is often depleted at the end of a day spent in intense encounter with other families. Emotional exhaustion coupled with the late hours required for a practice serving working couples, reduces one's availability to one's children. We regress, as Charny (1982) so aptly puts it, when we retreat to our own home and are likely to be less responsive to our children than we have been with our clients. My youngest child, in particular, has spent too much time alone as a teenager as a result of the late hours kept by both of his parents, a fact which he naturally resents. I often find myself torn between an event I wish to attend as his mother (i.e., a soccer game or band concert) and a patient in crisis. The stress on me at these times is equal to or greater than his disappointment. He does, however, take a certain amount of pride in his parents' professions, which balances the jealousy a little. He is able to rationalize that we are at least involved in life or death situations much of the time when we choose patients over him. Nevertheless, there remains an underlying anger that he is somehow being cheated. Experiencing this conflict makes me very sensitive to similar dilemmas of working mothers I treat, and motivates me to be creative in brainstorming solutions to the complications arising out of the multiple roles filled by today's women.

In spite of the factors working against us, because we are aware of the ideal in family functioning, therapists often strive for perfection and are not satisfied with "good enough." There is an overconcern about how our children appear in the community because their functioning serves as an example of our work. I worry about the role model I present to my clients and wonder if they think "If she can't keep her own house in order, why should we consult with her?" Anything done by our family in its position of prominence in our *small community* is subject to *public scrutiny*.

As therapist-parents, it is necessary to remind ourselves of our limitations. The emotional element can often cloud our decisions and behavior and we are frequently too close to a problem to see the solution. At times our unrealistic goals for our families put stress on all of its members and do not allow us to be human.

Most, if not all, of the pitfalls and assets of combining a career as a family therapist with raising a family of one's own, have been shared by other professionals I've known. Indeed, female students in the graduate program where I teach have established an official Women in Psychology Organization which serves as a support group dealing with these very issues. The fact that they have selected me as their sponsor and frequently consult me individually regarding my personal solutions to the conflicts arising from the multiple roles we live is testament to the fact that I *do* serve as a role model for them. I find that I am acutely aware of the very real complications faced by working women, whether students, patients or colleagues, in terms of raising a family and nourishing a relationship with their mates. My empathy is authentic and my suggestions realistic because I *too* have experienced first hand the complexities confronting today's women.

As I return to the scene at the pool deck, I am cognizant of the fact that my children are all highly social individuals with special talents. They appear to be fairly well individuated within our family system without being too disengaged. They each have their areas of strength and weakness. They have had their crises and difficult times and will have others in the future. My husband and I have "allowed" each other to pursue demanding careers while raising a family and sharing an active social life. We have passed through periods of closeness and separateness. We can list many successes, but there exist several areas of dissatisfaction. Nevertheless we have remained married for a quarter of a century in an age of divorce, providing our children with a secure, relatively stable home base, essentially free from unresolved conflict or intrusive closeness. We certainly are not perfect, nor are we very dysfunctional. We are a family experiencing the usual problems in intimate relationships, in living out our lives, counting more triumphs than failures, but certainly not trouble-free.

I take comfort in Charny's (1980) implication that the process of living will always include ambivalence and incompleteness and it is our adaptability, our learning to deal constructively with the vicissitudes of life, that matters. As he suggests (Charny, 1982, p. 50), we must not lose sight of the fact that "simply being, and enjoying being alive, is the central goal of existence."

REFERENCES

Bellack, L. & Faithorn, P. (1981). *Crises and special problems in psychoanalysis and psychotherapy*. New York: Brunner/Mazel.

Bowen, M. (1976). Theory in the practice of psychotherapy. In P. Guerin (Ed.), *Family therapy, theory and practice* (pp. 42-90). New York: Gardner Press, Inc.

Bowen, M. (1978). *Family therapy in clinical practice*. New York: Jason Aronson.

Bowen, M. (1981). The use of family theory in clinical practice. In R. Green & J. Framo (Eds.), *Family therapy: Major contributions* (pp. 263-311). New York: International Universities Press, Inc.

Carter, E. A. & McGoldrick, M. (1980). *The family life cycle, A framework for family therapy*. New York: Gardner Press, Inc.

Charny, I. W. (1982). The personal and family mental health of family therapists. In F. W. Kaslow (Ed.), *The international book of family therapy* (pp. 41-55). New York: Brunner/Mazel.

Charny, I. W. (1980). Why are so many (if not really all) people and families disturbed? *Journal of Marriage and Family Therapy*, *6*(1), 37-47.

Dalton, P. & Manning, M. (1986, March). *The therapist as parent. The parent as therapist.* Paper presented at the 9th Annual Family Therapy Network Symposium, Washington, DC.

Dinkmeyer, D. C., Pew, W. L. & Dinkmeyer, Jr., D. C. (1979). *Adlerian counseling & psychotherapy*. Belmont, CA: Wadsworth Publishing Co.

Ferber, A., Mendelsohn, M. & Napier, A. (1972). *The book of family therapy*. New York: Science House.

Framo, J. L. (1981). Family of origin as a therapeutic resource for adults in marital and family therapy: You can and should go home again. In R. Green & J. Framo (Eds.), *Family therapy: Major contributions* (pp. 341-373). New York: International Universities Press, Inc.

Freud, S. (1953). *Standard edition of the complete psychological works of Sigmund Freud*. London: Hogarth Press.

Ginsburg, H. & Opper, S. (1969). *Piaget's theory of intellectual development, an introduction*. Englewood Cliffs, NJ: Prentice-Hall, Inc.

Guerin, P. & Fogarty, T. (1972). Study your own family. In A. Farber, M. Mendelsohn & A. Napier (Eds.), *The book of family therapy*. New York: Science House.

Guerin, P. & Guerin, K. (1976). Theoretical aspects and clinical relevance of the multigenerational model of family therapy. In P. Guerin (Ed.), *Family therapy, theory and practice* (pp. 91-110). New York: Gardner Press, Inc.

Guldner, C. A. (1978). Family therapy for the trainee in family therapy. *Journal of Marital and Family Therapy*, *4*(1), 127-132.

Kaslow, F. W. (1984). Treatment of marital and family therapists. In F. W. Kaslow (Ed.), *Psychotherapy with psychotherapists* (pp. 79-102). New York: The Haworth Press, Inc.

Levinson, D. J. (1978). *The seasons of a man's life*. New York: Alfred A. Knopf, Inc.

Minuchin, S. (1984). *Family kaleidoscope*. Cambridge, MA: Harvard University Press.

Minuchin, S. (1981). Structural family therapy. In R. Green & J. Framo (Eds.), *Family therapy: Major contributions* (pp. 443-473). New York: International Universities Press, Inc.

Nichols, M. (1984). *Family therapy, concepts and methods*. New York: Gardner Press, Inc.

Nichols, W. (1968, April). Personal psychotherapy for marital therapists. *Family Coordinator*, *17*(2), 83-88.

Racusin, G., Abramowitz, S. & Winter, W. (1981). Becoming a therapist: Family dynamics and career choice. *Professional Psychology*, *12*(2), 271-279.

Satir, V. (1967). *Conjoint family therapy*. Palo Alto, CA: Science & Behavior Books, Inc.

Seeman, L., Weitz, L. & Abramowitz, S. (1976). Do family therapists' family ideologies affect their impressions of families? *Journal of Community Psychology*, *4*(2), 149-151.

Stuart, R. (1980). *Helping couples change*. New York: Guilford Press.

Vogel, E. & Bell, N. (1981). The emotionally disturbed child. In R. Green & J. Framo (Eds.), *Family therapy: Major contributions* (pp. 205-235). New York: International Universities Press, Inc.

Impact of Therapist's Personal Family System on Clinical Work

Philip J. Guerin, Jr.
Irene M. Hubbard

SUMMARY. The impact of the personal life of a therapist on his or her clinical work has received decreasing emphasis in the field of family therapy in the 1980s because of the increasing emphasis on short-term therapy and psychopharmacology. The authors believe that relationship experiences in one's own family are the basic training ground for the development of an effective family and/or individual psychotherapist. This paper presents three major areas of importance to a therapist's use of self; his or her basic level of operational autonomy, management of personal and clinical reactivity and personal enrichment–from family experience and therapist's own family (TOF) work.

THERAPIST'S PERSONAL FAMILY SYSTEM

A blend of art and science, therapy at its best is a unique combination of the therapist's professional training and his or her experiences as a human being–the family context from which he or she comes and the relationships formed as a child, adolescent and adult.

After World War II, as modern psychiatry shifted from its neurobiological foundation toward a psychoanalytically-based theory, the therapist became the primary instrument of intervention. The impact of therapists' own introjects, mechanisms of defense and emotional vulnerabilities on their clinical work became more obvious. The psychoanalytic model employed the concepts of transference and countertransference and personal psychoanalysis for the therapist to purify the use of transference as a clinical tool. Personal psychoanalysis was deemed essential to make therapists aware of the unconscious forces

---

The authors are affiliated with The Center for Family Learning, Rye Brook, NY.

within them that might interfere with a patient's progress (Greenson, 1968).

In the beginning of the family therapy movement psychoanalytic theory remained the major theoretical orientation (Guerin, 1976). Although at times awkward in their application, transference and countertransference concepts were used in family therapy as they were in individual therapy. Bowen, the strongest proponent of therapist's "work" in their own families made a major departure from his own psychoanalytic training and practice by proposing a theory and method of practice that would work to defeat rather than foster the development of transference. In its place he offered the concept of differentiation (the ability to remain neutral in an intense emotional field) and the therapist actively "working" on defining a "differentiated self" within his or her own family (Bowen, 1972).

Family therapists using an experiental-eclectic model often combine the idea of transference/countertransference with "Gestalt-type experiences" in an effort to refine the therapist's use of self (Nerin, 1986; Satir, 1967; Whitaker, 1976; 1982). Structural, strategic and behavioral family therapists have made little room for the variable of a therapist's personal relationship experiences and would appear to deem it generally irrelevant to therapeutic effectiveness.

More recent developments outside the family therapy field in biological psychiatry and psychopharmacology, combined with the widespread emphasis on short-term rather than long-term psychotherapy have greatly diminished the focus on the therapist's personal life experience as an important variable in how they later conduct the therapeutic process.

A review of the literature of the family therapy movement demonstrates this clearly. Family therapy books and journals from 1970 to 1980 contain many more writings and references to the therapist's own family (TOF) per year than do those published between 1980 and 1986. The dominance of structural, systemic and strategic models since 1980 may explain this fact as well as the reality of a decreased emphasis on TOF in training programs and workshops throughout the country.

The authors believe that relationship experiences in one's own family are the basic training ground for the development of an effective individual and family therapist. This bias is based on 25 years of teaching and clinical experience. The remainder of this paper will present three major areas that in the authors' experience have the most impact on a therapist's effective use of self within the context of family therapy. They are: (1) the therapist's basic level of operational autonomy; (2) the therapist's management of personal and clinical reactivity; and (3) the therapist's personal enrichment from the positive impact of family and the TOF experience.

THE THERAPIST'S BASIC LEVEL OF OPERATIONAL AUTONOMY

We hypothesize that the emotional freedom and operational autonomy of psychotherapists can best be measured by their level of differentiation and adaptive level of functioning within their own family system. This operational autonomy develops in the experience of understanding and reworking the intensely conflictual relationship triangles within one's own family.

Differentiation is a concept developed by Bowen while he was doing research on schizophrenia. He later refined it to include the full spectrum of human functioning (Bowen, 1978). This dimension is used to evaluate an individual or a family's baseline level of emotional and intellectual functioning; a yardstick to assess long-term psychological functioning, resilience in the face of significant stress, and accessibility to therapeutic intervention. It is not, however, a useful tool as a marker of short-term progress in either functioning or in therapy.

For this reason there is a need for a concept of self that is more easily measured in the short-term, and the concept of the *adaptive level of functioning* can be useful here. It evaluates the relative ability to maintain functioning in the areas of productivity, relationships, and physical and emotional well-being in the face of significant amounts of stress.

For example, a person faced with a certain amount of stress may have a high level of differentiation so that he or she suffers little emotional distress and therefore requires little conscious effort to maintain a given level of functioning. Given a greater level of stress that does create emotional distress, however, that person might need a significant amount of conscious effort to maintain functioning. The adaptive level of functioning is the ability to make that conscious effort. Thus, at a given level of differentiation a person might automatically handle *x* amount of stress without symptoms. An increase in his or her level of differentiation would enable him or her to handle automatically *x and y* amount of stress. That same individual might also be able to handle the same amount of stress without an increase in differentiation by consciously mobilizing the coping forces at his disposal – in other words, by increasing his adaptive level of functioning.

THE CASE OF JOHN – FACILITATING THE ADAPTIVE LEVEL OF FUNCTIONING THROUGH TRAINING

An example of the difference between differentiation and adaptive level of functioning is provided by the case of John, a fifty-year-old psychiatrist who first began family therapy training and TOF work at age 36. John began his supervision and TOF with two concerns. First, his relationship with his parents was, if anything, overly close, and impinged on his nuclear family and his work. Second, he also struggled with what he believed to be an inappropriate fear that one or both of his parents would die. In his TOF presentation he talked about how this fear was present from childhood and might in some remote way have been connected to the fact that both of his maternal grandparents had been orphans.

John also speculated that his choice of psychiatry as a career might have been prompted partly by his attempt to master his fear. The anxiety that his parents would die reached its peak when, as an intern in a Manhattan hospital, he experienced flash fantasies of being called to the emergency room to find one of his parents dead on a stretcher. He handled those fantasies by doing his medical residency hundreds of miles from Manhattan.

When John began his TOF work these flash fantasies were several years behind him, but even then an unexpected call from his brother would unnerve him. If one of his parents became even moderately ill, he would overreact, cancelling office hours to fly home. John found that this inappropriate anxiety seriously compromised his effectiveness when he did consults in the emergency room and about medical and surgical patients.

In monthly TOF presentations for more than two years, he and his supervisor worked on lowering his anxiety and decreasing his excessive sense of responsibility and omnipotence. He was instructed to raise the issue of his grandparents' deaths with his mother and her siblings; he also worked on bridging the cutoffs in his mother's sibling subsystem and began to discuss his fears about his mother and his father.

The major mechanism whereby John improved his adaptive level of functioning and correspondingly his clinical level of operational autonomy was by learning to operate the triangles within the personal family system in a more functional way. He focused on his primary parental triangle involving him and both of his parents, and his parent-sibling triangle involving his mother, his brother and himself.

The hypothesis that the supervisor developed about the first triangle began with the assumption that John's grandmother's loss of both her parents by the time she was age 13 created in her an above average amount of death anxiety and sensitization to loss and separation. Grandmother managed this in some measure through her connection with her oldest daughter Sarah, John's mother, to whom she either explicitly or implicitly transmitted this anxiety. In Sarah, an intense and emotional person, this took behavioral form in an overconcern that some disaster was going to befall her and/or her sons. She repeatedly admonished them to be careful and often attempted to control their comings and goings. John's father, and older brother, Bob, reacted to Mother's anxious behavior by distancing from her. This predictably increased her anxiety, fear of tragedy, and attempts at control. In her younger son, John, she found an anxiety sponge. He joined her in her worry about his father and brother and did what he could to protect her from worrisome information. He stayed connected with his mother and made major efforts to succeed in life, perhaps to distance her from her worries. His career choice may well have been an attempt to master the entire situation.

During the time of John's father's illness the structure in this triangle had John and his mother in an overclose relationship organized around their mutual worry about father. In addition, John carried out the job passed on to him by his father, "Keep Mother calm and happy." Father was distant from both of them.

In encouraging John to learn to operate this triangle with more flexibility and emotional freedom, John's supervisor suggested two key steps. The first was to research the impact on his mother of his great grandparents' deaths, and of his grandmother's early death at age 45 of cancer. This was to be done by establishing a connection with each of his mother's siblings and opening the issue of grandmother, her death, grandmother's parents' deaths and his relationship with his grandmother. The goal in this project was to demystify early death and separation by opening up communication about the events of the past and their possible connection with his present emotional situation. The hope here was that while John was going through this process, he might become able to distinguish between the irrational and the real around this issue.

An additional potentially positive by-product of this project would be an increase in the connection between John's mother and her siblings. She would have a broader support network and perhaps more relationship options in which to deal with her anxiety, thus freeing John of some of that responsibility.

The second key step was to narrow the distance with father and give him back his wife. John's coach encouraged him to increase the amount of relationship time he spent with his father and, as the anxiety diminished, raise the issue of his mother's anxiety and her consequent efforts to control other's lives. John knew that if he did this in a straightforward manner his father would quickly jump to her defense and close John out. John's supervisor proposed a course of action in which he would instead approach his father with two messages, one praising his father for how well he managed his mother's anxiety and the other requesting instruction from his father on how he might learn to do it better.

This maneuver might appear to be a "strategic invervention," and in some respects, it is. However, the difference is that the authors would view this move as one technique in a much larger scenario. The purpose of the technique is to surface process that can then be dealt with intermittently on a long-term basis.

In the second triangle brother Bob was distant from both John and their mother, who were again in an overclose position. Mother was critical of Bob, and displaced much criticism on Bob's wife, Martha. John would end up defending his brother and Martha. He was quite fond of both of them. He was instructed to move toward his older brother in an attempt to improve the connection and reestablish the natural hierarchy of older-younger brother. John attempted this by requesting advice from his brother on how to handle better Mother's criticism of him and her anxiety in general.

The outcome was positive. Eventually John could visit home with much less anxiety and take the unexpected phone calls more in stride. He expended as much conscious effort as was necessary to override the impulse to fly home and managed to give up an appropriate amount of responsibility to his competent brother.

Seven years after completing his family training John called his former supervisor and asked for an appointment to discuss the impact of his father's terminal illness on him and his work. They met four times in 18 months, as John attempted to stay connected with his father through his illness and death without getting overly responsible for his father's well-being or allowing the quality of his own clinical work to diminish. John managed himself and his relationship with his father and other extended family members in a highly functional way. His professional productivity slipped somewhat, but he flew home only at those times when it was appropriate for him to be away from work and more available to his father and mother. After his father died, John took up the work of functional mourning and family reorganization by working on the relationships with his mother, his brother and his children through focusing on the life and death of his father.

In nine years there were a total of 38 sessions. The question arises as to whether John's response represents an increase in his level of differentiation or simply an increase in his adaptive level of functioning. Probably it represents the latter. His ability to maintain his level of functioning was not accompanied by a significant decrease in his internal emotional distress. Rather, he limited his loss of functioning by skillfully managing high levels of emotional distress.

Four years later John again returned to his former supervisor. This time he was concerned about his 15-year-old son who was mildly depressed and doing poorly in school. John had been struggling with the problem for over a year without success and found himself almost as phobic about his son's well-being as he had been years earlier about his parents'. Flash fantasies of automobile accidents involving his son replaced the old ones about his parents, reinforcing the hypothesis that John's progress had been an increase in adaptive level of functioning rather than an increase in basic level of differentiation.

John reported that this work over 13 or 14 years had greatly improved his freedom to move within the relationship systems of the families he treated, especially when dealing with key triangles and issues of death and separation.

REACTIVITY

Coldness and indifference, emotional insensitivity, hostile and provocative words or behavior, intense relationship conflict on the verge of being out of control, violence, sex, death, gender issues, child abuse, intrusive parents, passivity, and manipulative behavior all are capable of stimulating a reactive emotional response in a therapist. This reactivity then can become manifested in the therapist's behavior toward one or more family members. Each of us reacts more intensely to some behaviors and issues than we do to others. The ones that precipitate our reactions have been termed our "clinical triggers." If researched thoroughly, a high percentage of these reactive responses can be traced to relationship experiences in our own families. In the following example the authors track the development of a family therapist and her management of a clinical trigger through four years of training at The Center for Family Learning (CFL).

DEFUSING STELLA'S REACTIVITY – HER CLINICAL TRIGGER ISSUE

Stella presented her genogram in her Level I supervisory group describing herself as the youngest of three siblings who was raised almost as an only child. Her brothers were several years her senior. In her primary parental triangle Stella was distant from her father, connecting with him mostly as a medical consultant around mother's health issues. Years of distance had eroded the relationship between Stella and her mother so that she was in an over-responsible position in regard to mother's health but lacked personal connectedness. Life threatening illness is an emotionally charged issue in any family. Stella's experiences in her family of origin intensified the potential for this to be toxic for her.

When Stella was a teenager her mother was diagnosed as having coronary artery disease. This did not interfere with her mother's ability to function, as her symptoms were minimal, but carried with it a potential threat of a heart attack. Both of Stella's maternal grandparents had died of arteriosclerotic conditions. Stella was urged by her father to help her mother so that Mother wouldn't overwork and have a heart attack. Stella was consciously invested in keeping Mother alive by being a proficient mother's helper. It was understandable that Stella chose nursing as a profession; this further reinforced her over-responsible position in her family.

When Stella left home to be on her own, her mother was hospitalized for the first time with symptoms of cardiac arrhythmia. Stella functioned as the family's authority on medical matters, denying her own fears and anxiety and reassuring her mother, father and brothers during crises. She was still in that position when she entered the Level I training at CFL.

Early in her first year of training, Stella presented a family for supervision saying that she was feeling very anxious about the mother who was to undergo open heart surgery. Stella was not aware that she was responding to this clinical family in much the same way she responded to her mother's heart disease. The woman in the clinical family had exceeded her life expectancy. She was born with defects of the heart which could not be surgically corrected in childhood. She and her family had been told that she would not live to adulthood. The woman had led her life without regard to long-term consequences as she literally did not expect to have to live with them. Her family had distanced from her and her irresponsible behavior. She was in a relationship with a man who was physically abusive towards her and her

10-year-old daughter born out of wedlock. She lacked a plan for living the rest of her life.

Stella presented the family's genogram and announced to her supervisor, "I have just six weeks to give this woman the will to live before her surgery." The supervisor's comment, "That's not your job," brought a flood of emotion to Stella as she realized the absurdity of her words and recognized the source of her anxiety.

Her supervisor helped Stella explore this trigger issue in the context of her own family. Stella's mother was a stoic who didn't complain, and her accuracy in reporting symptoms to a physician was poor. Her personality pattern, combined with her husband's mistrust of physicians, caused Stella's mother not to seek medical treatment until serious problems had developed. She then frequently required hospitalization. Stella's part in the process was to educate her father about medical care in an effort to foster his confidence in physicians, while making frequent trips to evaluate mother's health status. Meanwhile, her parents did not have a primary care physician whom they trusted, and Stella realized that this was part of what kept her own anxiety level so high.

Two interlocking triangles with Stella's oldest brother were involved in her over-responsibility. Her brother acted helpless around crises of illness and mother complained to Stella about her brother's lack of consideration. Father and brother were close; Stella was distant from both of them. Stella could not effect any movement in her primary parental triangle without addressing her relationship with her oldest brother, which was distant and conflictual.

In her supervisory group Stella was coached to back out of her over-responsible role around the issue of health. She was advised to let her mother know her vulnerabilities in order to fracture the image Mother had of her as a successful woman who had everything in life.

The second part of the TOF plan was for Stella to bridge the distance between herself and Father. Her supervisory coach decided that the way to a better relationship with her father was through her oldest brother. Since Stella had recently connected with his wife, her sister-in-law, finding a kindred spirit there, she went to work on her sibling relationship.

In an effort to reverse her over-responsible role in her primary parental triangle around the issue of Mother's health, Stella began to direct questions to her mother about her health. The new behavior broke the family pattern of not talking to Mother about her health lest she be upset. Stella began answering her father's medical questions with, "I don't know. Why don't you ask the doctor?" When father reported what the physician advised, Stella refrained from second-guessing the doctor and would say, "Sounds like he's got a handle on it." She also began to talk to her oldest brother about her anxiety about their mother's health.

Eventually her parents began to use the same physician and developed confidence in him. Mother got better at telling him about her symptoms, and Father got better at encouraging Mother to seek treatment early. As Stella's importance as medical expert diminished, her mother began to vocalize concern about Stella's health and lifestyle. Stella was able to tell Mother about her depression and follow her advice, which was to keep busy. She asked her mother to teach her how to sew, to take her mind off her depression.

The triangles between her oldest brother and each of her parents required that Stella move toward a more personal relationship with him. He disapproved of Stella's profession, believing women should devote themselves to raising their children and not pursue careers. Stella began to ask him for advice on child-rearing and confided to him her fears about mothering. He responded in a practical way by taking more of an interest in her children, which Stella appreciated. It made her reaching out towards her brother more natural and easy. As she worked on developing that relationship, she noticed that Mother's complaints about her brother diminished, and he was calling Mother more. But it wasn't until Father made a comment about Stella's handiness, the kind of praise he usually reserved for her brother, that Stella knew she had a chance of connecting with her father.

In her fourth year of training at CFL, Stella was once again faced with a clinical family that mirrored her own issues. A couple at midlife with an adolescent daughter sought treatment following the father's heart attack. The parents were concerned about the level of their daughter Karen's depression, and the father was concerned about stress activating another heart attack. Karen was trying to smooth anxiety around her father to reduce his level of stress, and thus keep him alive. The following is excerpted from the third session with the family, who were talking about what they expected would happen to each of them if Father were to die.

Therapist: How dependent is your life on your father's?

Karen: I don't know.

Father: I think she'll make it.

Karen: I'd have to, wouldn't I?

Father: I think it would bother her a lot. She spends a lot of time by herself. She'd just have more time to miss me.

Therapist: What do you think she would miss about you?

Father: I think she'd miss the fatherly talks. I try to explain things to her and give her a chance to answer. Sometimes she doesn't let me know what she's thinking.

Therapist: What do you think you'd miss about your father?

Karen: I don't know.

Father: I was just thinking back to my father and what I missed. It's just that there's a void, an emptiness there. The finality, someone who was there just isn't there anymore. It's funny, I used to say that my father was old. He died at 57 so you can imagine how old he was. I just remember like an emptiness, just an ache. He's just not coming back, that's how I felt about it. I don't think it's something a lot of people think about, how they are going to feel about missing somebody.

Therapist: You were younger than Karen when your father died.

Father: Not much, I was 16.

Therapist: You've already improved on your fathering.

Father: Yeah, still haven't gotten past 57 though.

Therapist: Did you have any sense of unfinished business with your dad, things you had wished you had said or done?

Father: Not until later. Later I missed him. Not right then, I was too busy. Keeps you from thinking about the things you're not supposed to think about.

Therapist: (to Karen) Do you think there are things you haven't said to your dad that you'd like to say?

Karen: There are things I don't say often enough.

Therapist: How much do you let him know you?

Karen: Not very much.

Therapist: Not much? You get kind of stingy about that, do you? Do you find that when you don't talk about yourself that your parents make assumptions about what you are thinking and feeling?

Karen: Probably.

Therapist: (to mother who is tearful) What are you thinking?

Mother: I'm just thinking about Karen. I really don't know her. She doesn't say what she's thinking and she tries hard not to say what she's doing.

What's going on inside her, I have no idea. Sometimes she's unhappy, lonely and sad. And I wish I could help her, but I can't because she won't let me in.

Therapist: What if she opened the door and said, "I'll make it my responsibility to be more knowable," but then your job would be to just get to know her, rather than tell her what to do or try to help her.

Mother: I'd like to listen. I'd like to know her.

Therapist: Do you think you know your mother well?

Karen: I know her better than she knows me.

Therapist: Is that because she is more open or you ask more questions or what?

Karen: No, she is more open. If she's sad about something she tells it, or if she's happy about something she tells it.

Therapist: What about your father, do you think you know him well?

Karen: Pretty well.

Therapist: So you're the mystery person in the family.

Karen: Somebody's got to be.

In this family the adolescent daughter was behaving in an overly responsible manner towards her father, trying to eliminate stress from his life. While focused on protecting her father's health she was silent about her own needs and vulnerabilities while becoming depressed. The process was similar to that in Stella's family around this issue, but Stella, as the therapist, was able to remain free from the emotional intensity and focus on the process in the triangle.

PERSONAL ENRICHMENT – THE POSITIVE IMPACT OF FAMILY

The tone of most articles about therapist's own family work would lead one to believe that therapists come to their clinical work compromised by the influence of their families of origin. Worse – in order to become prepared, the message seems to be that to do good clinical work, one must cleanse oneself from those negative family influences through TOF work. Both strengths and weaknesses are derived from one's family experiences and it is important to recognize both. As clinicians, we have a tendency to focus on pathology rather than searching for assets and building upon them.

For example, in the previously described case of John, from his mother he learned to never give up, no matter what the odds seemed to be. He remembered reading a Vince Lombardi statement "It's not never being knocked down that counts, it's how many times and the way in which you get back up" and thinking "Vince must have learned that from my mother." From his dad, John learned that not everything has to be made explicit. That people can say " I love you" implicitly in countless ways. He also learned of the strength that can be borrowed from a quiet, distant person who always seems to be there at the right time. In his TOF work John added an ability to better operate in the triangle with his parents, to be less reactive to their more "obnoxious" idiosyncracies and to keep his expectations oriented toward their assets, rather than their limitations.

The discussion of Stella focused on her clinical reactivity, traced it to her family of origin, and described her efforts to manage it through TOF work. In addition to her clinical triggers, Stella brought some positives to her role as a therapist which could also be traced to her family of origin. As the youngest, who was not taken seriously, Stella was able to raise emotionally charged issues in her own family without the system reacting with anger. Overtly, she was most often dismissed as making irrelevant noise, but her comments would often be followed by reduced anxiety and more openness in other family members. This experience directly influenced her style as a therapist and gave her a natural ability to operate in high anxiety fields without becoming intimidated, although she had a tendency to under-value her effectiveness, just as her family had dismissed her contributions.

In her TOF work Stella attempted to decrease her over-functioning around issues of health, an area where she was overly valued in her family and to increase her personal connectedness with family members. This allowed her a new sense of belonging and legitimacy in her family which changed her self-perceptions and freed her to take more interpersonal risks in both her family and her clinical work.

SUMMARY

John and Stella are but two examples of the clinical relevance of the therapist's personal life experiences. The flow between our roles as family members and family therapists is an open, multidirectional pathway. Both positives and negatives are brought to our clinical work from our families of origin. The making of a psychotherapist does not begin in formal training, nor does it end at completion of a training program, but rather comprise a lifetime of experiences that hopefully are integrated into a refined and responsible use of self. When that responsible and refined "clinical self" gets caught up in the reactive emotional process of a family in treatment in a non-productive way, it is important for the therapist to return to the basic training ground of his/her own family to find the pathway out.

REFERENCES

Bowen, M. (1972). On the differentiation of self. In J. Framo (Ed.), *A dialogue between family researchers and family therapists*. New York: Springer Publishing Company.

Bowen, M. (1978). *Family therapy in clinical practice*. New York: Aronson.

Greenson, R. (1968). *The technique and practice of psychoanalysis*. New York: International Universities Press.

Guerin, P. J. Jr. (1976). Family therapy: The first twenty-five years. In P.J. Guerin, Jr. (Ed.) *Family therapy: Theory and practice*. New York: Gardner Press.

Guerin, P. J. (1979). Family therapy style, art and theory. In E. Pendagast (Ed.) *The family compendium I*. New Rochelle, NY: The Center for Family Learning.

Nerin, W. F. (1986). *Family reconstruction: Long day's journey into light.* New York: W. W. Norton & Co.

Satir, V. (1967). *Conjoint family therapy*. Palo Alto: Science and Behavior Books.

Whitaker, C. (1976). The hindrance of theory in clinical work. In P. J. Guerin, Jr. (Ed.) *Family therapy: Theory and practice*. New York: Gardner Press.

Whitaker, C. (1982). The ongoing training of the psychotherapist. In J. R. Neill and D. P. Kniskern (Eds.) *From psyche to system: The evolving therapy of Carl Whitaker* (pp. 121-137). New York: Guilford Press.

Their Family/Our Family: Who Wins? Who Loses?

Sandra B. Coleman
J. Doreene Kaplan

SUMMARY. Women who maintain a family therapy practice while taking care of their own families face a constant stream of perplexing problems, conflicting priorities and difficult choices. This paper examines some of the practical issues of time management and economics as well as the emotional conflicts, looking at how they vary over family life cycle stages. While acknowledging that there are no easy answers to these dilemmas, the authors offer some possible considerations toward resolution.

The relationship between family therapy and feminism is gaining increased attention. As Goldner (1985a, 1985b) cogently argues, systems theory has not done justice to the heavy influence of social forces and history on the structure and roles of the family. She looks at the sexual politics that pervade family therapy, pointing out the implicit paradoxes associated with both genders, and carefully notes that the cultural shifts necessary to change the model of "male privilege and female masochism" are a function of a social upheaval, which Goldner believes is presently in process.

Further evidence of the interest in feminism and family therapy is seen in a recent issue of *The Family Therapy Networker* (1985) devoted to a discussion of the topic. Ault-Riché (1986) in *Women and the Family*, a volume in Aspen's *Family Therapy Collection*, explores women in relationship to specific pathologies, i.e., alcoholism, eating disorders and depression, as well as the minority roles of women, the training of family therapists as feminists, therapy with lesbian clients and several other salient topics.

Sandra B. Coleman, PhD, is Director, Family Guidance Center, Inc. and Associate Professor, Department of Mental Health Sciences, Hahnemann University, Philadelphia, PA. J. Doreene Kaplan, ACSW, is Associate Director, Family Guidance Center, Inc., Riverview Plaza, Suite 203, 33 River Road, Yardley, PA 19067.

The present article is a departure from the academics of feminism and family therapy. It is a nonscientific, experiential article written by women for women, focusing on the personal experience of being a female family therapist. Certainly many of the dilemmas discussed are androgynous – women do not have an exclusive on all of them. Male readers are welcome to read and react to the material. However, readers should be aware, as are the authors, that this is by nature a sexist point of view. Further, although the authors recognize and respect the need for more "hard" data, that is not the goal here. We encourage readers to understand the purpose underlying this article and to recognize it as a deliberate departure from the traditional academic approach.

Beyond the political and theoretical issues ensconced in the various schools of family therapy there are practical, commonplace dilemmas that confront female family therapists every day as we work with the families we call "our patients." A vast majority of the women who invest themselves in family therapy careers are also wives, mothers, divorcees, widows and single parents. Although never-married women also treat families, as do a large number of men in all categories vis-à-vis marital status, the purpose of this article is to focus exclusively on female family therapists who have been married and have children. The practical experiences of such women seem uniquely important and it is to them that we address our present ideas.

Because of the structure of society, we believe the dilemmas discussed in the following pages are both more prevalent and more difficult for women. Those of us who grew up in the '50s or earlier were reared to be wives and mothers and taught to place the highest priority on satisfying the needs and wishes of our family. Although younger women may have learned a somewhat less rigid definition of the female role, such basic social changes come slowly. This socialization as caretakers can enhance our functioning as family therapists, but it is emotionally demanding and presents many guilt-laden conflicts. Traditionally female tasks, such as child care, meal preparation and shopping, are interpersonal and nurturing and in many ways constitute an at-home continuation of therapeutic behaviors rather than a change of pace. If and when divorce occurs, child custody is most often awarded to the mother and as a single parent, she is faced with significant additional stress.

In contrast, although men also face family responsibilities, they have been taught that their primary role is that of breadwinner and they are thus given implicit permission to place the demands of work ahead of the demands of the family. Further, those nonvocational tasks traditionally assigned to men, such as working on the car and lawn, are (usually) solitary physical pursuits requiring minimal emotional output and thus are effective antidotes to therapist burnout. Divorced fathers are more likely to live as bachelors with limited parental responsibilities, therefore freeing many more hours for recreational activities. Our exclusive focus on women is not intended to imply that men do not encounter any of the same problems, but to reflect the reality that despite much social change, women still assume the major family responsibilities associated with the problems discussed here.

Feminists point out that a nonsexist theory of female psychology must look at women in context, taking into consideration the social forces which impact on her development (Fine, 1985; Mitchell, 1975; Parlee, 1979; Sherif, 1979). Current feminist thought also focuses on the need for women to embrace those qualities which are uniquely female rather than emulating men or ignoring our differences (Lerman, 1986; French, 1985). Family therapists also need to examine the impact of the emerging woman on her family context, as she struggles to change power hierarchies and take control of her life. As women who are family therapists we often feel mired in a multiple bind, balancing the influences and needs of our own families, our treatment families, our feminist beliefs, our professional identification and our feminine instincts. The latter is the most conflictual.

Both of the authors had a well-developed achievement orientation, as evidenced by the list of our accomplishments. But we have an equally strong family orientation and a need to embrace those parts of ourselves which are traditionally considered "feminine." Our own struggles to balance the many parts of our lives clearly affect our work with women in families. Helping other families express and cope with their feelings about mother demanding more power or going back to school forces us to deal with the reactions of our families to the adjustments necessitated by our careers.

CASE EXAMPLES

Therapists choose to work with families for a variety of professional, theoretical and personal reasons. For many, in addition to the professional challenge, family therapy represents an expression of a significant personal value, a strong belief in the importance of family in our own lives. Consider, then, the dilemmas faced by the female family therapist who is struggling to be a highly competent, loving wife and mother while maximizing her professional achievement potential. The issues vary somewhat according to her own stage in the family life cycle, as certain aspects become easier and some more difficult. The following sessions, drawn from the experience of the authors, are an introduction to some of the most salient issues.

The Young Family

> Martha and Bill have come to therapy with her depression as the presenting problem. Martha, an attractive 28-year-old mother of two young children, has a reputation as a gourmet cook and a willing volunteer for school functions. Bill, a distinguished looking 30-year-old high-powered businessman, looks bemused and slightly bewildered as his wife begins to talk.
>
> "I don't know what's wrong with me. I should be happy–I have everything I always thought I wanted, but I feel rotten all the time. Sometimes I blame it on Bill, that he is too wrapped up in his job and doesn't pay attention to me, but I know that's not fair. He travels a lot and doesn't get home before 8 or 8:30 most nights. By then the kids are starving and cranky and driving me crazy. I could feed them earlier but it's important to me to have dinner together. When Bill gets home he is exhausted and just wants to sit down with the paper and rest for a bit. But I've been with kids all day and want him to take over with them for a bit. I want to stay home with my kids, but I don't think Bill has any idea how hard a job it is! Some days I wonder why I ever went to college and what happened to that young woman who could write brilliant essays on Elizabethan poets. Now I have trouble writing a grocery list and don't use words over three syllables. I think my brain has turned to mush. I try to get Bill to talk to me at night, to have an adult conversation, but he has been with people all day and just wants to watch a little TV and go to bed. He doesn't seem to care how I feel."

Therapist's Thoughts

As I listen to Martha's lament, so like that of countless other young women who come into my office, I wonder how she would feel if our roles were reversed. My kids are at home with a new sitter–my regular one called in sick at 11:00 p.m. last night. Tommy, my five-year-old, has a sore throat and a fever. My heart ached at leaving him–he looked so forlorn. I wished I could spend the day doing those comforting things only a mother can do for a sick child. I considered staying home, but I had six appointments scheduled with other families who were counting on me to help sort out *their* problems. My son wasn't seriously sick but I still felt torn between who "needed" me more that day – my therapy families or my sick child. If I did stay home I would lose the day's income, and the budget is tight this month. Either choice was guaranteed to make me feel guilty. In some ways I can identify with Bill's desire to quietly read the paper without all that family interaction Martha wanted. Often after a day of working with families, with its enormous drain of emotional energy, all I want when I come home is silence. I certainly don't want to hear about the day's minor tragedies or be asked to "give" any more. What makes it more difficult and confusing is that another part of me wants to hear about their day. I often feel I am missing something important by not sharing first-hand the minor triumphs and crises of my kids' lives.

Some of these dilemmas are shared by all working mothers, while others are more problematic or unique to family therapists. The conflicting loyalties and the need to constantly juggle priorities is intensified by the highly personal, intense arena of family therapy. Staying home with a sick child is complicated when it means cancelling and rescheduling a full day's appointments, especially when the delay may interfere with the established therapy process. And if your income is dependent on therapy hours, the decision becomes even more complex. The conflict between helping others to become more effective parents and its accompanying drain of time and energy on one's own parenting often invokes a pernicious double bind.

The Adolescent Family

When children reach adolescence some problems have been solved by attrition or diminished in importance. Child care is not longer necessary, there are fewer afternoon school plays to attend and no pressure to be a room mother. As children become more independent they can assume responsibility for getting to baseball practice and the dentist. The days of arranging carpools around appointments or cajoling a stay-at-home mother to take an extra turn are over. However, there are new and perhaps more difficult problems and unexpected sources of fresh guilt. Again, listen to the contrast between the experience of a mother in treatment and the personal thoughts of her therapist.

> The Hill family has come to therapy because of 14-year-old Denise, who is a behavior problem at school and constantly fighting and defying her mother at home. Her 16-year-old brother Rick is reportedly not much trouble, while her 18-year-old sister Laurie is away in her first year of college. Ron and Judy, the parents, are in total disagreement over how to handle

the kids and spend hours fighting about them. As Judy starts to talk about the problem, the other family members act bored and uninterested.

"Everyone treats me like a servant in this family. No one listens or cares how I feel—they are nice to me only when they want something. I never thought it would be this way. I devoted my whole life to being a good wife and mother, always going to school activities, carpooling for baseball and scouts, and doing everything I thought was expected. I really enjoyed it when the kids were young; those were the happiest years for me. Now everything is a struggle and one of the kids is always angry. Rick has his driver's licence and is always bugging me for my car and gets mad when I turn him down. But my biggest problem is with Denise, especially her attitude. She is supposed to come right home after school, but she either comes dragging in late or brings a whole gang of kids with her, which she knows is against the rules on the occasional days when I'm not home. Right after school used to be a special time for both of us; she would talk about her day and we would enjoy being together. Now she acts like I'm prying into her private business if I ask 'How was school?' I miss those close times. I guess part of the problem is that none of the kids needs me so much anymore. Laurie is away at school, Rick is always out and will soon be gone, and Denise wants to spend all her time with her friends. *It's like I'm almost out of a job*. Ron is very involved in his career and all we ever do is fight about the kids. Sometimes I'm afraid of what will happen when they are all gone and it's just the two of us."

Therapist's Thoughts

I found it difficult to imagine myself in Jan's situation, even though our children are similar ages. I'm sure she would find it equally impossible to see herself in my position. Letting the kids have the car is necessary in my family. Working three nights a week, I am seldom available to drive them anywhere. I remember my relief when the oldest finally got his license and I could quit worrying so much about being their chauffeur. Right now I was hoping he had remembered to take his sister to the orthodontist. As for intimate mother/daughter after-school chats, my own daughter would be shocked to find me there when she got home. She knows exactly what she is allowed to do and always leaves a note about where she is going. But every so often I become acutely aware that this is all based on trust and I don't really *know* where my kids are or what they are doing much of the time. They are responsible and have never given me any serious reasons for distrust, but how can I be sure? I sometimes feel guilty about expecting so much independence and leaving them with minimal supervision. But as a single parent I don't have a choice – they are too old for a babysitter, and I need to maximize my income to support them and try to put something away for their college educations.

One of the difficulties during adolescence is the lack of supervision when parents aren't home, especially at night. When kids are young a sitter provides reassurance that someone is taking care of them. But what happens when they are too old for a sitter? Maybe they can take care of themselves, but without an adult there, trouble becomes more embraceable. As family therapists we know that teens still need parents to set clear, firm limits to help them control their impulses. But what good are limits if someone isn't there to enforce them? Sometimes when I am working to help parents take charge of an out-of-control teen I become painfully aware that my own kids are home alone.

When children are in their teens the financial drain can be enormous and a second income may become a necessity. Mother's job may well be the only way the family can afford extras like the "right" brand of sneakers, car insurance, or an occasional vacation, not to mention college tuition.

The Empty Nest

When children are safely "launched" and living independently, one expects to breathe a much-needed sigh of relief. All those years of juggling responsibility between client families and one's own and feeling guilty for not being at home with the children are finally over. One's career now appears free of the constraints of family life. An out-of-town conference is possible without worry about making arrangements for the kids. One can work as many nights as necessary without the guilt of child abandonment. But even then thorny issues present new challenges to our coping abilities.

> Dick and Marie are a young-looking professional couple in their forties who have sought marital therapy for help with several difficult mid-life issues, including the stress of dealing with their aging parents and the consequences of their decision to remain childless. They are clearly attached to each other and committed to the marriage, but Marie especially is having a difficult time with this stage of family life.

"I never expected to have so much emotional conflict at this stage of life. Dick and I put a lot of thought into the question of whether to have children, especially when I was in my late thirties and motherhood became a time-limited option. We have both felt comfortable with our decision and fully enjoyed our life-style. I have worked hard at my career, and Dick has been most supportive. I am now a senior vice-president and the only woman on the management committee in my company. There is even a chance that I might eventually become president. My position has brought a lot of professional recognition and allowed both of us to travel all over the world, meet exciting people and have some wonderful experiences. We have always been able to do pretty much what we want and to afford all the extras that make life comfortable. We have worked at having a strong marriage and have felt fulfilled.

"I really thought the struggles were finally over and it was time to sit back and enjoy the rewards. But now we have a new problem with our parents. Dick's father died two years ago and his mother needs a lot of help. Dick's sister does what she can, but she is a single parent and has her hands full working and taking care of here kids. Dick helps with house repairs and that sort of thing, but Mom never learned to drive and needs someone to take her to doctor's appointments, shopping, etc., and in my position I can't take that much time off. Now my own mother's health is starting to fail and she really can't live alone any longer. My brother's wife has made it clear that Mother can't live with them, so we are faced with a difficult decision. She really doesn't want to go into a nursing home, but I don't see how we can ask her to move in with us. My grandmother lived with us when I was a girl and I remember how my mother resented being tied to the house, taking care of her. I certainly can't leave a career I have spent so many years building up, but I can't abandon her either. We could hire help – we could certainly afford it – but what would that do to the life-style we have developed? *If I wasn't willing to stay at home to take care of a baby, how can I do it for my mother?* It seems like a dilemma with no right solution. It has also prompted me to think about what will happen when Dick and I get old – there will be no children to take care of us or worry about what happens to us. When we were making our decision not to have a family, I really never thought about the consequences for our old age."

Therapist's Thoughts

I can empathize with Marie's feelings since we are in a similar stage of life. However, I have three children in addition to being a full-time family therapist and spent most of my adult life juggling the two roles rather than concentrating on one, as Marie has done. Listening to Marie talk about her career success and glamorous life, I felt some envy and was aware of the compromises I made in my own career to accommodate my family life. Now my children are finally grown and I have more time to devote to work, but it is too late for some of the things I might have achieved. Conversely, sometimes I also feel a pang of regret that I devoted so much time and energy to may career when my children were young. It seems their childhood passed so quickly and I missed too much of it. They have turned out fine—healthy and independent adults who are well equipped to deal with their lives. I don't feel sorry for them, but perhaps for myself. There are times when I wonder if I had the best of both worlds or the worst, if by trying to have it all I missed out all around. I also understand Marie's resentment and conflict about the demands of aging parents. My mother has been in a nursing home for over a year, and I'm still dealing with my own guilt and her anger that I couldn't take here into my home. I try to visit as frequently as possible, even though I have so little free time. When she had pneumonia last winter, I was constantly calling the doctor to make sure she was taken care of properly, calling her several times a day, and visiting the hospital whenever possible. All this was sandwiched between my appointment hours and other responsibilities.

MAJOR CONFLICTS FOR THE WOMAN FAMILY THERAPIST

As demonstrated in these vignettes, there are many conflicts imbedded in our work with families. Some are logistical, such as trying to accomplish forty-eight hours of work in a twenty-four hour day, while balancing work responsibilities with family demands. Others are financial—finding a way to adequately support a family, either alone or with a spouse, without basing all your decisions on money. Even when the practical issues of time and money are under control, the emotional conflicts may overwhelm the female family therapist as she struggles with parental guilt, emotional depletion and burnout. And choosing priorities is an ever-present issue. Although our own family may clearly be our top priority, sometimes they must take a backseat when a treatment family "needs" us more on a particular occasion.

Time Factors

One of the most obvious areas of struggle in our commitment to both treatment families and our own is the allocation of time. All working mothers know there are never enough hours to accomplish all the required tasks. However, there are also specific contingencies for a family therapist.

The scheduling of treatment hours is a major problem. Family therapy frequently necessitates late afternoon or evening hours. When attempting to work with four or more family members who are either in school or at work it is not realistic to label their inability to assemble in a therapist's office at 10 a.m. as a "resistance." Thus, families are usually seen at night – the prime time for us to be with our own families.

Evening work has some intrinsic value when children are quite young, as it permits us to be at home during the major portion of their waking hours. However, marital benefits are minimal since couples usually see each other only in the evening. This clearly imposes hazards on the therapist's marriage, subjecting it to vulnerabilities beyond those of couples who have similar working hours. How paradoxical that the more successful the therapist becomes in helping couples resolve their differences, the more likely she is to work more hours, imposing more stress on her own marriage.

For the single parent, the demands of evening work are enormous. She often has to arrange childcare during a portion of the day as well as at night. When she is free at night, time with her youngsters is essential, leaving little time for her own important socializing. As a "9-to-5er" she could be with her children several evenings and still have time for herself. As a family therapist there is an inevitable crunch that devours night time opportunities for relaxation, meeting friends, dating and activities that help one avoid the burnout factor that infects those who work with emotionally upset people.

When a divorced mother becomes seriously involved with a man, she may have to face a modification, if not a real shift in her career. How formidable a situation she would create for herself and her children when she remarries if she spends 50% of her evening hours away from the adjustments associated with the reconstitution of her family. If a natural father resents being at home alone with the kids too often, imagine the feelings of a new stepfather. On the other hand, if she makes a dramatic change in her career, her resentment may well have a pernicious effect on her new marriage, creating another set of dilemmas and anxieties which can invade all facets of her complex life.

When the single parent's children are grown and out of the home, some of these problems disappear. However, after many years of only limited participation in social activities, she is often isolated and a stranger to a single's social world. She may have to go through an enormous amount of personal change to adapt to the single scene, which at mid-life may be less than desirable for someone new to this experience.

Single or married, the time demands of being a female family therapist are filled with conflictual issues. Clearly, the rewards are such that most of us find ways to cope and we do survive. It is important, however, that the factor of time is recognized. Without attention to these limitations, beginning family therapists in particular are apt to become victims of timebound situations that restrict their personal development and ultimately prevent them from enjoying their own family lives.

Economic Factors

Contrary to the belief of clients, family therapy is not a highly lucrative field, particularly when one considers the hours spent outside the session on phone calls, contact with referring agencies and schools, studying videotapes, consulting with staff, etc. Many of the rewards are intellectual and emotional; the remunerative value fluctuates and is often not the major professional benefit. Although the prospects of becoming rich as a family therapist are not great, one can certainly earn an adequate living if one does enough therapy hours. Differences prevail depending on the practice setting.

Private Practice

The earning potential is probably greatest in private practice where fees and hours are self-regulated, *if* sufficient referrals can be generated. However, this advantage is offset by the irregularity of income and the need to grapple with many conflicting loyalties. There is no such thing as a consistent paycheck, and winter's snowstorms and summer's vacations that interfere with patient appointment schedules can wreak havoc on a therapist's budget. While income may fluctuate wildly from week to week, a family's needs do not. This is particularly problematic for the single parent, whose children don't eat less just because she had too many cancellations. Nor does the mortgage company care about the slow insurance payments in January. Without a steady income from another job or a spouse's employment, the private practitioner needs strict discipline in money management. There are none of the usual benefits such as paid vacation, sick leave, health insurance, pension plans or disability payments that one receives in academe or in an agency setting. She must also pay her secretary, rent, office phone bills, postage, photocopying costs and all the other expenses of running a practice. The overhead traditionally absorbed by an institution is her costly responsibility, even when business is slow or she is out sick.

These factors impose heavy pressures on us all, but the strain falls most heavily on the single parent. There is also a constant stream of difficult choices. For example, a major dilemma is whether to be with one's children one more evening or to bring home needed income from another night in the office. This conflict is not resolved once and forgotten – the "right" balance changes throughout the family life cycle, as children grow older and their needs change. A young child may need less economically and more emotionally and physically, while an adolescent may enjoy the independence of time alone but need to know there will be money for his/her college education. Certainly the woman who must support herself and her children is in a more untenable situation than the one with a spouse who contributes additional income. Despite the disadvantages, however, private practice offers women an opportunity to earn adequate money, function with maximum autonomy, avoid double standard pay scales and male-dominated promotional opportunities, and achieve some degree of flexibility to shift hours to accommodate family demands.

Agency Practice

In contrast to the financial fluctuations of private practice, working in an agency provides a regular paycheck. Unfortunately, that paycheck will likely be for less than needed. While agency pay may improve, the nature of social service funding ensures that it will never be competitive with earnings in the private sector. Choosing to work in an agency generally means accepting that the pay will always be relatively low; consequently one's ability to provide funds for one's family will be comparatively limited. Whether the advantages make this an acceptable alternative depends on one's financial situation, stage of family life cycle development and priorities. For women with families this all too often creates perplexing conflicts.

Emotional Factors

Our education and training as psychotherapists seldom provide ample preparation for how emotionally draining it can be to spend one's working hours dealing with the problems of other people's families. Regardless of theoretical orientation, therapy requires empathy, emotional availability and a level of personal involvement which can leave one feeling depleted and empty. As therapists we are constantly exposed to the pain of others, and as human beings we cannot avoid being affected. Experience teaches us to keep a certain professional distance and maintain a boundary between our clients' problems and our own. But this distance can be bridged and we often suspect the boundary is an illusion. Family therapy in particular invokes a sense of the kinship among all humans struggling to negotiate the turbulent waters of family relationships (Ferber, Mendelsohn & Napier, 1972). The stress of this work can lead to therapist burnout, a feeling of emotional depletion often accompanied by anxiety, depression, irritability and psychosomatic complaints (Jayaratne et al., 1986). There is an increasing body of literature on this phenomenon, including some studies which have examined the effect of burnout on the therapist's family and found that high levels of burnout are associated with increased marital stress (Cray & Cray, 1977; Farber, 1983).

As female family therapists we are well aware of the impact of our own emotional burnout on our families. After a long day/evening of giving to others, sharing their pain and anger, controlling our own emotions to better help our clients, we are often left feeling exhausted and emotionally spent. But as wives and mothers we come home to families who also need our emotional involvement and have a right to expect us to be available. At times it seems everyone wants "a little piece of me" and that if it were possible to give everyone what s/he wants there would be nothing left. This is a particular problem for women, who are taught to be responsive to the needs of those we love and put them ahead of ourselves. Violating this dictum may invoke intense guilt and personal questioning. As mothers we want to be there for our children. But this may not be easy if one's teenage daughter is upset about a tiff with her friends, while you are emotionally reeling from a session with a family whose thirteen-year-old daughter is sexually abused by her stepfather. As family therapists we know the importance of keeping the lines of communication open and that if we constantly turn her away with the "little things," she may not come to us when she has a "big problem." "Can we talk about this later?" can be used just so many times before she begins to feel less important to us than our clients. This is one "trap" identified by Charney (1982) in his discussion of the family mental health of family therapists.

When we are juggling taking care of client families with taking care of our own families, the person who gets shortchanged may be us. One of the traits most therapists share is being more comfortable giving to others than asking to have our own needs met. If one is constantly giving without getting replenished, feelings of emptiness and resentment may well prevail.

ADVANTAGES FOR FEMALE FAMILY THERAPISTS

The impact of a career in family therapy on one's own family is not all negative. One advantage is the perspective derived from our inside view of how other families function and the often creative ways they find to solve their problems. Knowing that all families struggle with particular issues can be very reassuring and promote a healthy outlook on our own struggles. Although helpful at all stages, this awareness reaches a peak of importance when our children are adolescents. As family therapists we know first-hand that teens need to rebel. When our own children choose nondestructive acting out behaviors to handle their conflicts we are more able to assess and accept the situation realistically because of what we see daily in our offices. When our husbands are upset over the kids' messy rooms or lack of diligence in doing chores, our professional exposure can help them to see these as normal and necessary acts of rebellion.

Another advantage we gain is a preview of family life stages in our own futures. Seeing other families struggle with issues we have yet to face allows us to foresee and prepare for the stage-relevant tasks. The potential pitfalls are seen first-hand in our work. When we help couples cope with their empty nest stage, we learn the importance of strengthening our own marriages and developing more mutual interests before our young adult children leave home. When we help a woman come to terms with her guilt and grief over unresolved conflict with her deceased mother, it encourages us to deal with our relationships with our own living mothers.

Our work may also provide an understanding of emerging patterns and contemporary issues. Current adolescent stressors become apparent, exposing us to the realities our own children are facing. If we live and work in the same community we may learn quite specifically about conditions in local schools and social networks. Working with couples also provides an inside view of common marital issues and patterns. We may gain a perspective on our marital relationships and perhaps a new appreciation of our husbands. Listening to other couples, we often come home feeling grateful for the men we married.

TOWARD RESOLUTION

The issues we raise are not new or unique. The problems inherent in the field for women therapists are evident and every woman can readily underscore the impact they have on her individually and on her family. Their resolution of these problems, however, is complex and no universal rules apply. Each woman's situation must be understood within its own idiosyncratic context. Some general coping strategies, however, may be delineated.

Individual Consideration

Each woman needs to explore her personal needs which are left unmet by the crunch of career and family. So much of the time we are caught in the perpetual motion of schedules and responsibilities. Time for self-reflection becomes a rare luxury. Nevertheless, such introspection is an essential function; once we acknowledge and identify the source of our frustrations we can begin to make some modifications.

Many women find their lives to be a seesaw between career and family with no balancing point in between. Sometimes only another activity offers that balance. Although this may seem paradoxical it is not an attempt to generate "more of the same." Only if a woman finds a self-nurturing outlet for the stress of always being in the bind between "their family" and "our family" is she likely to avoid succumbing to some physical or emotional problem herself. This third arena or balancing point is most productive when it is not emotionally laden but is in marked contrast with the other things we do. For some it may be a physical activity such as a sport or health club that energizes and provides the needed revitalization. Perhaps a creative interest such as photography or painting may help to release pent-up frustrations. One's choice of a *third environment* can change according to the seasons, unlike our families and careers which often take on too much familiarity with too few seasonal fluctuations. Regardless of where a woman's interest lead, it is therapeutic to have at least one segment of her life that does not demand that she give, listen or problem-solve. That freedom from the expectations of others should be the criterion she uses for selection.

Family Considerations

To suggest that the family therapist have a "session" with her own family may meet with resistance. Often the last thing a family wants is for their wife/mother to "do her thing" with them. However, like the shoemaker's barefoot kids, our own families may lack the open communication that we encourage in our treatment families. Our spouses or "significant other" and kids need to know about our personal struggles. If we can share our frustrations and worries with them instead of trying to be "superwoman," we keep our loved ones aware of our pressures. When we keep them on the inside track in a compassionate way they are better able to cope with the effects our work schedules and stresses have on them. This helps to ease their reactions to our absences and lapses in emotional availability when we are present. Certainly this is more productive than short-tempered outbursts and unfair, non-giving reactions to their needs or requests when we feel over-burdened and tense.

Beyond open discussion we need to plan family fun times that we truly enjoy. We may want to participate in some activities such as Little League, Brownies and Scouts, etc. as part of our parental responsibility. However, it is important to find family activities that we and our family can sincerely take pleasure in sharing together. All too often, because we are so busy during the week working outside the home, weekends and holidays are spent "catching up" with work inside the home. No real time exists for much else and fun is usually omitted. If we could learn to change our expectations of ourselves and perhaps our standards of housekeeping and put fun ahead of work more often, we could substantially improve the internal disorders that we suspect families of family therapists are most apt to suffer.

Career Considerations

One of the most difficult tasks we can undertake is the honest self-exploration of our career goals and needs. Being a family therapist along with being a wife and mother is complex. Because the field is still relatively new, most of us have had many years of formal training in other disciplines prior to studies in family therapy. When we finally became graduate family therapists we were highly energized to succeed. Few of us want to let up. Like someone eating peanuts we become obsessed with learning "just one more" new technique, reading the latest brilliant book and attending the conferences that will guide us forward into the land of the wizards of family change.

Sometimes we work too hard in our efforts to succeed professionally and become frenetic about preventing any traditional gender role from smothering us. Because we link being female with many years of patriarchal servitude and second-class citizenship we often forget the unique joys and wonders our biology can bestow. We rarely "fast forward" into the futures of our own family lives, forgetting how quickly one stage catapults onto another. We need to project a split-screen image of the family life cycle and career life cycle. Yet it is this conflicting vision that upsets us. For, is this not our ever-present dilemma? It is part of the struggle feminists face, a struggle imbedded in the controversy of political turmoil. Perhaps Marilyn French (1985) says it best when she states, "The major problem facing feminists can be easily summed up; there is no clear right way to move." Although French is not referring specifically to the career vs. family issues central to this discussion, her masterful study of power clearly underscores much of what we are saying. French concludes her volume with a look at the future, suggesting that, "The starting place is within the self, in an investigation of our needs and desires, a reconsideration of what gives us pleasure, what makes living seem desirable; and of our pursuit of power or control."

A SPIRITUAL SOLUTION

French views integration of one's total personal capacities with those of the world as essential. When she discusses the blending of the private and the public worlds she approaches some of the ideas expressed in Spretnak's edited volume, *The Politics of Women's Spirituality* (1982). Spretnak herself suggests that we adopt the holistic, integrative, spiritual approach. She, somewhat differently from French, sees the "theme of women's elemental power" as represented by "many moments in a woman's life wherein she gains the experiential knowledge, in a powerful body/mind union, of the holistic truths of spirituality." The Goddess spirituality of which Spretnak writes is described as "a symbol of the holistic nature of life on Earth."

Jean Bolen's (1984) view is that there are many "goddesses" within every woman. "The more complicated the woman, the more likely that many are active within her. And what is fulfilling to one part of her may be meaningless to another." Bolen believes that women must become aware of their inner goddesses as well as the outer forces of society and its role expectations of women which "reinforce some goddess patterns and repress others."

Perhaps if we become aware of the many goddesses within us we can learn to express what they represent at varying times in our own life cycles. The integration of the influences of our goddesses may ultimately be the way we find our own internal answers. The views of French, Spretnak and Bolen offer us hope and provide us with support for journeying inward, for in fact, this is the only solution there is.

REFERENCES

Ault-Riché, M. (1986). *Woman and the family*. Rockville, MD: Aspen Systems Corporation.

Bolen, J. S. (1984). *Goddesses in everywoman*. San Francisco: Harper & Row.

Charny, I. (1982). The personal and family mental health of family therapists. In F. Kaslow (Ed.), *The international book of family therapy* (pp. 41-55). New York: Brunner/Mazel.

Cray, C. & Cray, M. (1977). Stresses and strains within the psychiatrist's family. *American Journal of Psychoanalysis*, *37*, 337-341.

Farber, B. A. (Ed.) (1983). *Stress and burnout in the human service professions*. New York: Pergamon Press.

Ferber, A., Mendelsohn, M. & Napier, A. (1972). *The book of family therapy*. New York: Science House.

Fine, M. (1985). Reflections on a feminist psychology of women: Paradoxes and prospects. *Psychology of Women Quarterly*, *9*, 167-183.

French, M. (1985). *Beyond power*. New York: Ballantine Books.

Goldner, V. (1985). Feminism and family therapy. *Family Process*, *24*, 31-47 (a).

Goldner, V. (1985). Warning: Family therapy may be hazardous to your health. *The Family Therapy Networker*, *9*, 18-23 (b).

Jayaratne, S., Chess, W., & Kunkel, D. (1986). Burnout: Its impact on child welfare workers and their spouses. *Social Work*, *31*, 53-59.

Lerman, H. (1986). From Freud to feminist personality theory: Getting here from there. *Psychology of Women Quarterly*, *10*, 1-18.

Mitchell, J. (1975). *Psychoanalysis and feminism*. New York: Vintage Books.

Parlee, M. B. (1979). Psychology and women. *Signs*, *5*, 121-133.

Sherif, C. (1979). Bias in psychology. In J. Sherman & E. Beck (Eds.), *The prism of sex: Essays on the sociology of knowledge*. Madison: University of Wisconsin Press.

Spretnak, C. (Ed.) (1982). *The politics of women's spirituality*. New York: Anchor Books. *The Family Therapy Networker*, (1985), *9*.

How to Be Sane and Happy as a Family Therapist or The Reciprocal Impact of Family Therapy Teaching and Practice and Therapists' Personal Lives and Mental Health

Florence W. Kaslow
Norma Schulman

SUMMARY. There is no doubt that the issues of the personal and professional life of the family therapist intertwine. The complicated process through which the therapist, as a person, must filter his/her own experiences is predicated upon and enhanced by the roles of clinician, teacher/trainer, and supervisor/consultant. In this article this reciprocal impact is examined. Suggestions are made as to how therapists can remain or become emotionally and physically healthy. Given what the field knows about the personal and professional lives of family therapists, the implications for training of fledgling practitioners are considered briefly.

The complex interrelationship between the elements of the therapeutic process, the transitions and transactions of the families with whom one works, and the therapists whom one supervises, and one's own personal life and significant others are constantly interacting and influencing their respective outcomes. From the importuning of Socrates, "Know thyself," (Socrates, 1937) through the posturing of Polo-

Florence W. Kaslow, PhD, is Director of the Florida Couples and Family Institute and in independent practice in West Palm Beach, FL and Adjunct Professor of Medical Psychology in Psychiatry, Duke University Medical Center. Norma Schulman, PhD, is a psychologist and family therapist and is in independent practice in West Palm Beach, FL and serves on the Board of the Florida Psychological Association.

nius, "to thine ownself be true and thou canst not then be false to any man" (Shakespeare, 1602), the demand for self-awareness and the conscious use of self pervade the intellectual experience of the conscientious therapist and clinical trainer.

The unfinished business of the past within the therapist's own family of origin, his or her own emotional responses and psychological associations, memories, and fantasies may well be stirred up in intense contact with patient families. To avoid projecting one's own struggles onto patient families, we believe it is important, even imperative, that family therapists have explored their own genograms (McGoldrick & Gerson, 1985) and either made voyages home to resolve perplexing relationship issues from childhood (Bowen, 1978) or participated in therapist-led multigenerational family therapy sessions to achieve the desired resolution and acquire the know-how for continuing to improve family of origin ties instead of resorting to "cut offs" (Bowen, 1978). Trying to keep one's personal family of origin and family of creation relationships highly satisfying and functional, attending to the numerous and complex demands and needs of patients, as well as fully discharging the responsibilities to those the educator trains or helps toward professionalism, may rapidly become a heavy burden.

Concern for the well-being of patients, and for maximum efficiency and effectiveness in training and supervising others, have led us to review the many stresses that can impede – may even damage – the well-being of family therapists themselves. The involvement in helping individuals in patient families to co-evolve into self-actualizing and still cooperating, healthier people, sometimes within, and sometimes apart from, their nuclear family units, can illuminate our path to doing the same so that we also recognize the need to make a major investment in sustaining and improving our own physical and mental health.

THE DAILY WORLD OF FAMILY THERAPY

Stresses and Strains

The everyday world of the therapist encompasses dealing with the demands of one's patients, trainees, students, supervisees, and colleagues, among others. Implicit in the work environment itself are concerns about having enough patients, students, supervisees and/or securing ample research funds, getting enough publications in refereed journals, being involved in professional and community organizations, and collecting patient fees, royalties and honoraria. In this decade, concerns about malpractice and liability and the cost containment thrust of HMOs, EAPs and PPOs that may lead to reduction in quality of care and a shrinkage of the patient flow for independent practitioners all converge to contribute to incredible stress and press, both internally and externally.

The very nature of the "therapeutic personality" often makes it difficult for the therapist to say "no" and the constant pressure to overextend one's self is difficult to resist. For some professionals hoping for entreé to prestige and power in their professional field, the ambition to build a fine reputation, coupled with the demands of building a practice and the need for success must be monitored carefully if they are to avoid chronic discontent, burnout, and even breakdown (Freudenberger, 1983). Today we are much more cognizant of the fact that therapists, like everyone else, are vulnerable to distress and impairment and that helping professions, like psychology, must address identification and treatment of impaired mental health practitioners (Kilburg, Nathan & Thoreson, 1986).

Importance of Patient Goals and Values

Even while we grow to appreciate the extent of our own knowledge and understanding of individual psychosexual development, the family life cycle, family systems dynamics and life experiences, recognition must also be given to the idiosyncratic values and lifestyles of client families. No matter how much the therapist believes in such principles as women's liberation, feminism, equalitarian marital relationships, and children's rights, patient families need to be seen in the context of *their* own ethnic patterns, religious convictions, family traditions, socioeconomic and educational experiences, as they are, not as we would want them to be. They come to therapy to clarify and achieve their objectives. We believe that although it may at times be tempting to do so, we cannot superimpose our ideal of the perfect or happiest kind of family on them as our goal for their therapeutic outcome. We may introduce new ideas and options for their consideration, and by so doing influence their thinking and behavior, while still respecting *their* right to determine what is important to and for them.

Distressing Syndromes

Beyond the development of skill in establishing rapport, improving one's understanding of families in difficulty, and mastering intervention strategies, the clinician must also address the effect of the demands placed on his/her psychological well-being as a therapist by the same issues that bring families into therapy. Chronic or terminal illness, accidental death, substance abuse, suicide, homicide, divorce, severe economic reverses and myriad other problems all impact on the practitioner and his/her personal family as well as on families in treatment.

When faced with cases which encompass incest or child abuse, the therapist must follow the legal requirement to report suspicion of abuse. Such reporting to authorities is often in conflict with one's professional commitment to confidentiality, the doctrine of patient privilege, use of informed consent forms, and one's personal code of ethics and morality. Filing a suspicion of abuse report with the designated agency may disrupt the all too fragile therapeutic alliance. The desire to help rectify a dysfunctional pattern by establishing a trusting relationship in the safe sanctuary of the therapist's office may conflict with the duty to report to authorities. Somehow these apparent contradictions must be kept in a sometimes precarious balance.

The Shadow of Malpractice

In the decade of the 1980s, the spectre of a malpractice suit hovers all too near, causing an undercurrent of anxiety. Rates for liability insurance are mounting steadily as patients become more litigious. Mental health professionals have become fair game as their incomes have risen. Given that many patients enter therapy with unrealistic expectations of becoming better and functioning beautifully—within a brief time span—and given that many of them exhibit poor impulse control and can enter into a negative transference (or a disgruntled blaming of the therapist for their "failures") if they do not get their way—we are becoming increasingly vulnerable to the frustrations and disappointments of our patients being worked out in courts of law instead of in the non-adversarial context of our offices. Recently a prominent judge told author F. K., "You'd be wise to consider every patient who walks through your office a potential adversary. . . . There are scads of lawyers specializing in personal injury and malpractice cases who actively seek clients who are discontent with the results of treatment." What a chilling and disconcerting quandary this now poses for all of us!

Even if the clinician is certain he/she is innocent, the insurance company (and/or one's own legal counsel) may suggest trying to reach an out-of-court settlement and to not risk the trauma of a trial and the possibility of a jury verdict of guilty, with the accompanying high damages to pay. To the innocent therapist, often naive about the tangled web of processes utilized in the justice system, such reasoning is unfathomable. A settlement seems an admission of guilt. Yet, preparing for and going through an accusatory trial looms as a horrendous ordeal. In small cities and towns such trials may be open to the public and sometimes receive unwelcome press coverage. For clinicians who believe therapy is a private endeavor, only to be shared with colleagues with full patient knowledge and approval, such exposure to the public is at best unsettling, at the worst, an embittering and totally noxious experience. Thus, we have found that even if one goes to court and is exonerated from the charges, the process itself of being deposed and on trial is extremely destructive to the therapist and his/her family.

Repeated Terminations

Termination of each therapy is inevitable. More than any other professional, therapists must continually deal with the reality of termination. Whether intervention has been successful or not, the ending of treatment is often experienced as another separation and sometimes with a sense of loss. The patients are people whose lives we've "joined"; now it is time to exit from their system – permanently. Despite one's professionalism, one may still experience ambivalence at closure of a case.

Endings are often complicated as one trains others, and relationships are transformed from teacher/student to supervisor/supervisee to colleague. Former students become friends (Friedman & N. Kaslow, 1986). In small towns, former patients become acquaintances; therapist-patients are seen in various professional contexts. This experience of non-closure and transformation can be a source of additional stress or a source of satisfaction, depending on the teacher or therapist's capacity to feel free to make decisions with regard to personal preference about the nature of any posttreatment relationship. It may also make the therapist or trainer more sensitive to "losing" members of his/her own family, such as when older adolescent and young adult children "move out" to go to college, get married or simply to live away; or when faced with the impending loss of a spouse or parent. They may have already experienced too many partings. Caring and investing in others lives can indeed come to feel very risky.

SEPARATION OF PERSONAL AND PROFESSIONAL ROLES

Recognition of the separation of one's personal and professional roles and space in life, allowing ourselves to be "just another member of a family," rather than "an expert," can help us to avoid (1) the excesses of a full-time caretaker role, and (2) antagonizing other family members because of a supercilious attitude. Nonetheless, we need to balance our personal lives by utilizing what we have learned that is appropriate with regard to the nourishment of our own personal relationships with our children, our significant partner, friends and relatives. Communication skills, problem definition and strategies for problem solving, a sense of positive regard, consideration and an open emotional expressiveness, albeit learned or enhanced through professionalism, can certainly be utilized "at home" and in social situations.

In insidious ways, personal family life may sometimes be threatened by continuing professional growth, evolving work satisfactions, and in-depth close relationships with fellow professionals. For example, in striving to achieve excellent working relationships with co-therapists, co-teachers, collaborators, colleagues, or consultants, a therapist may ultimately share much more of his/her inner self – working on "becoming" in a co-evolving relationship. The co-therapy (or co-teaching pair) may come to exercise great integrity and great honesty with one another, evolving a high level of trust, respect and affection (Rice, 1986). As they get to know each other well, sharing realms of cognitive and affective experience, they may come to feel closer to and more understood by their daytime partner (the co-therapist) than by their nighttime and weekend partner (the spouse). They can find a wonderfully stimulating and gratifying synergic buildup of energy, productivity and fine therapy results from their tandem efforts. If they are having difficulty communicating as fully and in as great depth with their mate, and if their marital partner is not particularly interested in their professional activities and thoughts, the marriage may pale in comparison, seeming far less exciting and rewarding.

Trainee and Patient Admiration – Does the Family Share It?

Some patients and trainees are very expressive of their admiration. This may be flattery, positive transference and/or genuine recognition of the therapist's knowledge and skill. If one is on the speaker's circuit, doing guest lectures near and far, and attains something akin to "guru" status, invitations and adulation abound. For some, it is hard to resist believing in the myth of their own "greatness." They replay their precious videotapes over and over, with each new audience looking on adoringly and the therapist as film star, like Narcissus, falling somewhat in love with his/her own image. Reinforcement of one's talent and "specialness" is particularly potent when one is voluntarily sought out by other therapists for supervision and consultation (Kaslow, 1986a).

The contrast between one's professional success and tangible signs that one is appreciated and valued may be, therefore, all the sharper and more worrisome when the attributes that lead to professional stature, satisfaction and rewards carry little weight within one's own family. When the therapist's own family resents the time, energy, attention, and involvement given to others (who are perceived as strangers), then the resulting competition and dissatisfaction can challenge not only one's credibility but even one's sense of accomplishment and professional dedication.

One's workaday worldly success may impede one's ability to relate to one's own family, particularly if the therapist craves the same intensity of interaction, adulation, focused attention to communicating and problem solving and relating with his/her significant others that he/she experiences in the office or classroom. Conversely, if the therapist/spouse/parent goes home emotionally depleted from the demands of "being on" and "tuning in" all day, the family may well assume and then resent that more energy and caring seem to be available to patients than to them. Family members, knowing one's weaknesses too well, can quickly remind us of our own fallibility, and powerlessness, by acting up, acting out, and thoroughly frustrating our sense of competence and accomplishments. One may be capable of enabling other families to function much better, but the more he/she tries to tinker and tamper with his/her own, the more resistant they sometimes become. In our own families, we are or should be participating members, not objective, intervening therapists.

Competition and Comparisons

Complications develop if the therapist compares treatment couples/families to his/her own marriage/family and perceives a competition between them (Charny, 1982). The problems within one's own family of origin, like never having received unconditional love or sufficient expression of approval and recognition, if utilized as a comparative yardstick and depending on the measure, may cause the therapist to feel insecure, confused, uncertain, disgusted, angry or complacent. Seeing client families become successful in resolving issues and solving problems, and thereby becoming healthier, can be viewed with mixed feelings. Disappointment and frustration abound when the therapist's own family continues to experience disruption or disharmony and resents and resists his/her efforts to have them deal with their difficulties—taunting him/her "don't play shrink with us." Some therapists seem to inevitably compare the trauma and disruption in their own personal lives to experiences in the lives of their clients and trainees. Given the virtues of empathetic and compassionate effort, it is obligatory that the therapist/consultant guard against inappropriate overidentification, overintellectualization, or becoming too much a part of the patients' lives and allowing concern for or intrigue with them to spill over into his/her at-home world.

Recurrent and typical themes in family therapy are intense in their impact, and often are disturbingly similar to those themes in the therapist's own life. These include concerns with individuation and separation; loss and grieving; ambition and striving; dependence and independence; belonging and connectedness. Family issues regarding personal development; autonomy, co-evolution and self-esteem; and the universal emotions of anger, hurt, desire for retaliation, and longing are the oft repeated foci in treatment of families. It is inevitable that these concerns, although they make take different forms or vary in intensity within any given family group, will reverberate back onto the therapist. The patients' successful or nonsuccessful resolution influences the therapist's perception of self as competent or incompetent in both the personal and professional spheres of his/her life.

Confidentiality Concerns

The basic professional principle of confidentiality may pose a problem for the therapist's own family as it dramatically conflicts with fundamental assumptions about open communication in the family and has endless ramifications for all involved. Therapists should not talk about patients; their identity and concerns must be kept "secret" from the clinician's family. The family may perceive this impenetrable veil of mystery as a curtain that shuts them out; there is a whole part of wife/mommy or husband/daddy's world that they are not entitled to know. (When a therapist works with a valued co-therapist who does share this world, the jealousy and resentment may be intensified.) One can come home perplexed by a troublesome case and is restricted from discussing it. This is atypical in other vocational fields, a person can come home and use his or her spouse as a sympathetic listener or sounding board. Thus, the therapist's spouse may be the recipient of the frustration and yet be unable to learn about or understand its source or to be empowered to do anything to offer relief through catharsis.

At times, particularly when one practices in a small town or within a small group of identifiable individuals, one must be especially vigilant about protecting client identity. Some therapists rarely socialize in their home towns in order to avoid potentially embarrassing situations; this can restrict their spouse's social life and may cause additional resentment and tension.

Several examples of the complexities professional interactions pose for personal life with consequences for one's spouse will be given to illustrate.

Shortly after author F.K. moved to the Palm Beach area and began seeing patients, she had the following dialogue with her husband:

S.K.: Our friends, the Cs, will be visiting from Philadelphia and would like to go out with us for dinner this weekend.

F.K.: Super. I'd love to see them.

S.K.: There will be a third couple who also recently relocated here. Mr. C thinks he and I can be extremely helpful to one another in business and I've been waiting to meet him.

F.K.: Sounds fine. I hope we click, as I still feel somewhat socially isolated. What's their name?

S.K.: They are the Js.

F.K.: (Gulp. The Js are patients of hers.) Oh, I forgot. We're already busy!

S.K.: What? You rarely forget and you're acting strange. (Looking closely at wife for cues and seeing the veiled look he can identify) I guess that means you can't go out with them! (Pause.) This really poses a problem. How can I now decline and tell them no evening is good when I initially indicated how pleased we would be to join the four of them? Why must your professional commitment demand such rigidity and sometimes impose unfair restrictions on the rest of the family's social life?

There are no simple solutions. When the pair are a dual career couple, the kind of situation cited above may not be atypical. The couple must decide which relationship is primary. In the instance cited above, the therapist spouse was already involved with couple J. The businessman husband of the therapist agreed to arrange to meet Mr. J. through their mutual friend at lunch, minus their respective wives, so they could establish their own potential collegial interaction.

When a therapist's children are growing up, it is not unusual for the following sequence to occur:

Monday evening

Teenager: Mom and Dad, is it all right if I have some friends from school over for a party Saturday night? It's the usual group you know, plus their dates. They're all very nice.

Mom: Sounds okay. We can be here and help out, if you'd like.

Saturday night

Bobby: Hi, Judy! Hi, Don. Oh, Hello, Dr. R. I didn't realize Judy was your daughter (somewhat sheepish at having blurted it out).

Dr. R. (Mom): Hello, Bob. Welcome. You look well.

Judy: (quietly) Please don't feel embarrassed, Bob. Everyone here knows my folks—one way or another—so I doubt anyone else will realize how you might know her.

It becomes apparent that the therapist must convey the nature of his/her work to family members and explain why confidentiality and protection of patient identity are important. Then family members can also devise ways to quickly pick up cues, as in the vignette above, when contact with patients occurs unexpectedly, and be able to contribute to the smooth handling of a situation so it doesn't become too awkward, revealing or embarrassing.

When professional experience creates a sense of frustration and disappointment, because of resistance, therapeutic plateaus, and "stuckness," the therapist may carry home disgruntled, negative attitudes. Creative problem solving, a sense of humor, and even a sense of the absurd on the part of the therapist and his/her significant others can be most helpful. An awareness and respect for the rhythm and pace of families, oftentimes unlike one's own, and quite different from one's own personal rate of growth and learning, can be enhanced by the therapist's recognition and acceptance of other people's uniqueness. A humble sense of perspective and a view of one's self as a catalytic agent and facilitator/guide, rather than as a supposedly omnipowerful, omnipotent, and all responsible agent of change, can be a soothing and beneficial attitude at difficult times and one which helps prevent severe stress and ultimate burnout.

The Spectre of Violence

An issue of increasing distress to many therapists and their significant others is the number of cases with which they deal in which someone is quite violent. We are aware that the violent patient is not confined to the mental hospital or prison, where there traditionally have been some built-in protective features like guards, other staff members on the ward or cell block, and some training in containing violence and self-protection. Volatile and dangerous patients and their victims (abused spouses, children, parents, live-in partners) come for help to public welfare agencies, shelters for women, hospital emergency rooms, family service agencies, and private practice offices. Many therapists, until recently, were not trained in recognizing and confronting the violence in family systems and in realizingthat, if they did not handle this eruptive undercurrent skillfully, they too could become a target. Several years ago, a female psychiatric resident at the University of Wisconsin was murdered by a male outpatient in her office at the Medical School. In June 1986, author F.K. was lecturing at the Post Graduate Family Therapy Program at Tel Aviv University on "The Self of the Therapist" to a group mourning over the fatal stabbing of a social work colleague the day before. The social worker had been helping a pregnant patient to leave her abusive husband and move toward divorce. Following a court order restraining his behavior, the irate and panic stricken husband came to the therapist's office, armed, apparently intending to kill his wife. In the ensuing moments, the social worker intervened in an effort to protect her patient. The husband killed both his wife and the therapist.

Practicing today involves hours of immersion in families that act out their frustrations and anger in physical abuse. Being surrounded by the threat of dangerousness can be quite frightening (see May-June, 1986 issue of *Family Therapy Networker* for excellent coverage on "Lifting the Shade of Family Violence"). Expression of this fear by patients and by therapists may once have been overinterpreted as paranoia or immaturity; yet all too frequently, the fear is well-founded and we realize our's is not really such a low risk profession. Our parents, spouses, and children may worry about our safety. And so may we. This can diminish our pleasure in work. It is rarely possible to "enjoy" families that present severe dysfunction that includes substance abuse coupled with violence. Some clinicians go home after hours filled with such patients, feeling depleted and pessimistic. Instead of being available to our loved ones, we may feel so exhausted that all we want to do is retreat into sleep, TV watching, jogging or some other noninteractive, nondemanding activity. Family members come to feel, if this is a repetitive scene that we (1) care more for our patients than for them, (2) are not "fair" in our allocation of time and emotional energy, and (3) are inconsiderate in causing them worry while shutting them out. Indeed, there are days where it is neither easy, interesting, nor fun to be a member of a therapist's family!

RECOMMENDATIONS FOR ACHIEVING BALANCE

Therapy for the Therapist

As a physician is urged to "heal thyself," therapy for the therapist can be a source of maintaining one's maximum satisfaction with professional life, and extending one's capacities for continuing professional involvement indefinitely. Sometimes a touch of narcissism, grandiosity, and/or omnipotence makes it difficult for therapists to set aside their competitive and rivalrous strivings and turn to another for help. Some fear that their identity and problems may be revealed and/or that the therapist they might confide in will believe that if they are having severe problems, they should curtail practice. Fears that the therapist might today feel compelled to report them to a peer review or ethics committee may inhibit self-disclosure (Kaslow, 1986b). Others had thought that they "completed" therapy years ago and see needing to return as a sign of weakness or failure. It is ironic that some of those who make "doing therapy" their life's work and who, in other realms of their living, attest to its efficacy, are so reluctant to avail themselves of this healing and revitalizing experience.

The choice of a therapist by and for a therapist/patient (T/P) is never simple (Faye & Lazarus, 1984). It becomes even more complex if the therapist/patient is well-known, lives in a small community, has a "secret" the disclosure of which might endanger his license or cause great damage to his reputation because it would require reporting. Extensive examination of the selection of a therapist and of the preferred treatment modality and philosophy have been discussed elsewhere in detail, as have the distinctions between supervision and therapy to which we continually address ourselves, so these will not be repeated here. (The interested reader is referred to *Psychotherapy with Psychotherapists*, F. Kaslow, Ed., 1984.)

Treatment for the Therapist's Family

At times, the necessity may arise for involving the therapist's own family in family therapy. In some training programs, this practice has become an extension of the training program itself. One may argue on both sides of this question. On the one hand, the therapist's sensitivity, awareness and experience can be greatly expanded by such a process. One learns the terrain of the inner world of the family and what it's like to sit in the patient's chair—disclosing innermost thoughts, dreams and fears, in front of one's relatives. Family therapy may be much more emotionally taxing than individual therapy; there is no room to hide, no way to obfuscate. One gains respect for patient resistances, cautions, outbursts, etc. from "being there." Yet, others argue that therapy for one's own family implies unrealistic expectations of solving all one's family problems and may ultimately lead to further disappointments and disillusionment. A few, like Haley (1976), believe it is irrelevant and may impede, not improve, one's therapeutic skills.

Beyond the training context, a desire to deal with and ameliorate family dysfunction may be the reason for entering therapy. While some family members may resent and resist the therapeutic process for themselves, others may develop a finer appreciation of the professional role and responsibilities of the family member who is the therapist. The therapist and his or her spouse's own parents and parenting behaviors will come to be reassessed, and their family of procreation's issues will be reworked, often in the direction of making peace with one's family of origin and improving the functioning of the current family.

When issues are more intrapsychically based or related to one's professional world rather than the interpersonal family realm, then individual or group therapy may prove to be more appropriate therapeutic modalities than family therapy.

Networking

It is not always necessary or advisable to enter or reenter therapy when one is troubled by professional concerns. Our profession has certain inherent protections that each one of us can utilize and renew consciously, as often as needed. The therapist need not practice in isolation; rather one can establish a network of contacts to provide different options for support, clarification and additional learning. Occasionally, the most obvious method is the use of a co-therapist or a behind the one-way screen team. These approaches enable one to have a colleague present (1) to share the "burden" in a very difficult case, (2) to help bail one out if he/she has become enmeshed in the family system or involved in a negative counter-transference, or (3) to break an impasse in the therapist/patient system.

The seeking out of high quality supervision or consultation can provide support to and the illumination of the disciplined, conscious use of self by the therapist, a reactivation and maintenance of the observing ego, and a different view of patient dynamics and functioning. Presenting audio or video-taped sessions and soliciting critiques from valued colleagues, or if one is in solo independent practice, from other professionals in a peer network, can be most beneficial. Keeping current through attending professional conferences and workshops and relevant reading are also helpful.

Transferring Patients

Another option when one is completely "stuck" is to make a decision to transfer an extremely difficult case, difficult because it is prolonged, chronic, falls outside the therapist's areas of expertise, or because the therapist/patient match is a poor one that they are unable to work through. Such a transfer can be interpreted as a sign of strength and wisdom, not of weakness and inadequacy. As therapists, we can not be all things to all people and we are prohibited from practicing beyond our area of competence (APA, 1981).

In addition, when a patient is struggling with issues so close to the therapist's current life experience that the therapist finds it too painful and stressful to deal with these at home and in the office concurrently, issues like terminal illness of a close family member or grieving over a recent death or divorce, nonacceptance or transfer of a patient(s) is preferable to undertaking or prolonging a therapy in which one becomes overly involved and cannot handle one's own too positive or too negative counter-transference. Such a referral represents a sensitive and humble awareness of one's limitations and the placing of the patients' needs for efficacious treatment above one's own for a busy therapy schedule.

Upgrading Skills

One's ongoing effort to maintain high standards of performance by continuing to read, attend workshops, and critique one's own work alone or in tandem with a supervisor/consultant (Kaslow, 1986) enables one to bring their knowledge and experience to bear to help others. Ultimately, this leads to respect and appreciation from at least some of one's clients, trainees and colleagues, a sense of one's own competence, and refreshed and revitalized intervention strategies.

Personal Care and Replenishment

The physical side of one's life must not be overlooked. Given the typically sedentary and confined nature of therapeutic practice, the wise therapist includes in his/her life attention to exercise and physical fitness, personal care, rest, medical and dental appointments, and social activities that are fun. Personal pampering, such as a body massage and/or visits to the hair salon, are vital to a sense of well-being, as are both brief and extended vacations. Time alone and with significant others, without the stress of problem solving, is essential. Reserving times for one's personal needs and pleasures reflects a resolution of one's need to be needed and oftentimes signifies readiness to accept that appropriate expectations of one's self do not include overwork and omnipotence. A good work-play balance and emotional giving and receiving are as vital in the therapist's life as in the patient's.

Unfortunately, the tendency to develop a pattern of overload begins early in one's training as a family therapist. The unrealistic expectations of one's self require not only short-term utilization of professional consultation and even treatment, but an awareness of pacing and scheduling that depend upon a disciplined use of time and a sense of priorities. Simply put, daily schedules must allow break time for unwinding, exercise, being with friends and loved ones, building in likely success experiences, avoiding scheduling one's most difficult cases back-to-back or on one day, and the availability of a "coffee pot."

In addition, principles and pacing are reflected in variations in the nature of professional commitments. Training, teaching, lecturing, writing, attending or giving workshops, in addition to clinical practice, continuing education experiences, and involvement in nonprofessional realms of life can greatly enhance one's views and resourcefulness. The sense of excitement and stimulation that arise from variation allow for renewal of an optimistic perspective, and thereby enhance one's functioning rather than distracting from one's sense of purpose. And, such assorted activities are worthwhile in and of themselves, not as justification, but as part of "being" and self-actualizing.

Disengaging from One's Professional Role

The mature professional learns to "turn off" so that he/she can more thoroughly enjoy and be enjoyed as "a person," without his/her professional biases, and to interact comfortably in social situations, so that he/she can have the opportunity to be rejuvenated while relieved of the demands and burdens of the professional stance. Personal relationships are of great value in enhancing and nurturing the therapist, just as they are for one's students/clients. Learning how to receive love, affection and emotional sustenance from others, allowing one's self to be taken care of and being able to enjoy playfulness may require a conscious effort on the part of the therapist to relinquish in-charge behaviors. The demands of graduate training programs, as well as the expectations of one's continuing growth in professional performance make relaxing control a most difficult experience, *and* a most vital one.

In some situations it is a matter of avoiding superhuman behaviors. Such simple measures as arranging for assistance with ordinary household chores, and in the professional setting, insisting on and/or providing oneself with adequate and competent secretarial and other office staff and support systems, is essential. An attractive and secure office environment is a necessary requisite to the enhancement of one's safety and sense of well-being.

Warning Signs

How does one know that he or she is entering a danger zone when there are no signposts marked "high stress or burnout area straight ahead"? In our therapeutic work with distressed professionals (Kaslow, 1986b), some of the early warning clues noted are:

1. not wanting to go to work;
2. constantly complaining about disliking practice or feeling overwhelmed by it;
3. sense of foreboding or "imminent doom";
4. life seems dull, heavy and tedious;
5. experiencing an increasing number of negative counter-transference reactions to patients or students;
6. being extremely irritable, withdrawn, depressed and/or intolerant at home;
7. suffering frequent illnesses of inexplicable origin;
8. wanting to "run away" from it all or having periodic suicidal ideation.

When two or more of these symptoms appear periodically, and with increasing frequency and intensity, the therapist or trainer has entered a twilight warning zone and should probably enter therapy, take a vacation of several weeks duration, cut back practice for a while until he/she feels less overwhelmed, *and* perhaps consider a shift in focus with his/her career.

IMPLICATIONS FOR TRAINING

In the training of family therapists, as well as other mental health professionals, the need for consciousness raising in the development of sensitive awareness to one's own needs as well as those of patients goes beyond substantive material and skills training. Perhaps a clear statement about legal and ethical codes which govern practice in the requirements for graduate programs is where the beginning must be made. In those programs where personal and/or family therapy is required, or recommended strongly, this too needs to be considered in light of all of the advantages and disadvantages such personal experiences can provide.

Descriptions of and discussions about the lifestyles of family therapists are a must; does the trainee really want "the whole package"; can his or her family accept it? Issues of potential danger in the field must be addressed, as must the potential to be sued and subpoenaed. Ample opportunities to discuss student fantasies, motivations and apprehensions must be provided by skilled teachers, supervisors and consultants. Readings about the self of the therapist can be assigned.

The issues of burnout and stress, the demanding toll that training as well as ongoing professional effort take on the individuals who become involved, is not as simple a matter as urging medical students to be vaccinated against life-threatening diseases when such vaccines are available. Simple or not, our responsibility in training professionals is no less vital. Our concern with the health and well-being of our field cannot be addressed in an abstract form and in an intellectual discussion. Trainees need to learn how to avoid stress and burnout by taking care of themselves and we can model no less. Encouraging attention to physical fitness as well as to clinical learning appears important if one is to be a healthy therapist. If we profess a concern with the health and well-being of others, our responsibility to ourselves is equally salient.

NOTE

1. Taken from comments made by Jay Haley at a workshop for supervisors of family therapy at the Philadelphia Child Guidance Clinic in 1976.

REFERENCES

American Psychological Association. (1981). *Ethical principles of psychologists*. Washington, D.C.: American Psychological Association.

Bowen, M. (1978). *Family therapy in clinical practice*. New York: Jason Aronson.

Charny, I. (1982). The personal and family mental health of family therapists. In F. W. Kaslow (Ed.), *The international book of family therapy* (pp. 41-55). New York: Brunner/Mazel.

Charny, I. (1986). What do therapists worry about. In F. W. Kaslow (Ed.), *Supervision and training: Models, dilemmas and challenges* (pp. 17-28). New York: Haworth Press, 1986.

Family Therapy Networker (May/June 1986). *Lifting the shade of family violence*. Washington, D.C.

Fay, A. & Lazarus, A. (1984). The therapist in behavioral and multi-modal therapy. In F. W. Kaslow (Ed.), *Psychotherapy with psychotherapists* (pp. 1-18). New York: Haworth Press.

Freudenberger, H. (1983). Hazards of psychotherapeutic practice. *Psychotherapy in Private Practice*. *1*(1), 83-89.

Friedman, D. & Kaslow, N. (1986). The development of professional identity in psychotherapists. Six stages in the supervision process. In F. W. Kaslow (Ed.), *Supervision and training: Models, dilemmas and challenges* (pp. 29-50). New York: Haworth Press.

Kaslow, F. W. (Ed.). (1984). *Psychotherapy with psychotherapists*. New York: Haworth Press.

Kaslow, F. W. (Ed.). (1986a). *Supervision and training: Models, dilemmas and challenges*. New York: Haworth Press.

Kaslow, F. W. (1986b). Therapy with distressed psychotherapists: Special Problems and Challenges. In Kilburg, R. R. , Nathan, P. E. & Thoreson, R. W. (Eds.), *Professionals in distress: Issues, syndromes and solutions in psychology* (pp. 187-210). Washington, D.C.: American Psychological Association, 1986.

Kilburg, R. R. , Nathan, P. E. & Thoreson, R. W. (Eds.) *Professionals in distress: Issues, syndromes and solutions in psychology*. Washington, D. C.: American Psychological Association, 1986.

McGoldrick, M. & Gerson, R. (1985). *Genograms in family assessment*. New York: W.W. Norton.

Rice, D. G. (1986). Supervision of co-therapy. In F. W. Kaslow (Ed.), *Supervision and training: Models, dilemmas and challenges* (pp. 119-142). New York: Haworth Press.

Shakespeare, W. (1602). *Hamlet*. In Shakespeare Volume II. (1931). New York: Scribner's Sons.

Socrates (1937). From Xenophon's Memorabilia of Socrates. In *The classical moralists*. (Compiled by B. Rand). Boston: Houghton Mifflin.

The Family Life of Psychotherapists: Treatment and Training Implications

Joan E. Winter
Harry J. Aponte

SUMMARY. An exploration of the relationship between a therapist's clinical effectiveness and his family life, illustrated with a transcripted series of interviews with a therapist, provides the foundation for the development of a clinical training model. The process of family resolution and the management of the therapist's personal characteristics and subsequent utilization in the therapeutic context is examined. The *Person/Practice* model is aimed at schooling self and changing self to enhance the therapeutic outcome.

A therapist brings to his* work the heritage of his past family experiences and the effects of his current family functioning. In every therapist there is a unique set of personal and familial themes and memories which are the family myths that are, "fairly well-integrated beliefs that are shared by all family members" (Pillari, 1986, p. 6). These themes are drawn from the history of the person and his family, his ethnic origins and sociopolitical legacy as well as the family's current social context. The events which mark a person's life, including both past and present, are inextricably connected and serve as an interpreter and guide to his life.

In combination with a therapist's historical roots, he lives in a current familial and societal context which also introduces into his ther-

Joan E. Winter, LCSW, is Director, Family Institute of Virginia, 2910 Monument Ave., Richmond, VA 23221. Harry J. Aponte, ACSW, is Director, Family Therapy Training Program of Philadelphia, 1420 Locust St., 32-D, Philadelphia, PA 19108.

The authors wish to express their appreciation to Grace J. Haded, LCSW, Training Coordinator, Family Institute of Virginia, for the technical assistance and administration skills she contributed to this article.

The trainee Jay has agreed to have his story told. His identity is somewhat disguised for his protection.

*"He" is used throughout since the trainee being discussed is male. No sexist implications are intended.

apy the influences, themes and developmental issues of his contemporary relationships. Structures and patterns from his present life and familial context also govern how the therapist interacts with clients. The familial currents of past themes and present structures are, by nature, intertwined. The past molds the present, the present is used to reinterpret the past, and therefore, alters the impact of the past.

For a clinician to effectively use himself within the therapeutic context, he must attempt to understand his own family, past and present, and resolve issues that trouble him and hamper his functioning. As Kaslow asserted, when therapists had resolved their personal issues "their energy did not remain bound up in these struggles but became available for learning and clinical tasks" (1984a, p. 86). Lack of such resolution, as indicated, limits a therapist's ability to not only grasp or conceptualize issues within his or her clinical cases (thinking), but it also obstructs a clinician's capacity to conduct actual therapeutic interventions (acting).

A therapist's own family is the incubator for the development of relationship skills. Considering the point that the development and use of the therapeutic relationship is still the only reliable predictor of positive psychotherapy outcome (Gurman & Kniskern, 1981), the family's effect on the therapist's ability and comfort in relationship development is vital.

In brief, lack of resolution of a practitioner's family issues hampers his ability to think, act and relate within the therapeutic context. The development of the person of the therapist, and his resolution of familial issues, is integral to successful treatment outcome.

Understanding and changing himself are not enough, however. The therapist must learn how to translate these gains into the actual conduct of therapy. Within the therapeutic context, a clinician deals not only with the systemic forces of the present transactions, but also vicariously with his own family issues in the problems clients present to him (content) and in the therapeutic relationship (projection).

This indirect, vicarious process inevitably brings to the surface both the resolved and unresolved aspects of his life. Thus, it is essential for the practitioner to learn to recognize and manage the flaws and scars of his life since there is no possibility that he will ever achieve full resolution of current or past affiliations (Freud, 1964). Seeking to resolve personal dilemmas is a lifelong challenge. Although the clinician's efforts are aimed to "achieve a degree of resolution in his personal life, in all circumstances it will mean knowing how to manage within the therapist his reactions to unresolved personal issues in ways that will benefit the client" (Aponte & Winter, 1987).

Clinical training serves the function of linking these two arenas together: the therapist's personal self with his therapeutic self, i.e., the part of the clinician which he utilizes within the treatment context. An exploration of the effects of the practitioner's own family dynamics on his subsequent, and interlinked, conduct of treatment provides a fundamental component for the development of treatment and training methods.

An examination of the effects of two key dynamics of the family of origin and the family of procreation which impact upon the therapist, illustrated by a transcribed case example, as well as the consequent treatment and training implications, provides a framework for inquiry. This exploration illuminates the vital bridge between the therapist's conceptual understanding and conduct of treatment, and his families of origin and procreation.

FAMILY OF ORIGIN: UNIT OF IDENTITY

Each person's family of origin becomes the formative culture or environment where the child's view of himself and the world is originally shaped. Thus, the family of origin is the *unit of identity* where the person's initial view or "trance" with regard to himself is formed. Carl Whitaker once observed that all people are in a hypnotic trance for the first several years of their life (1982). The early formation of one's identity and world view is critical and perhaps, some would hold, even ever-lasting. This seems particularly true of those experiences that occurred before memory became an operational brain function (usually prior to three years old). Certainly, Freudian analysis was predicated on the impact of the child's early years and the effect of the family on the development of self (Freud, 1957). Successful therapy, to one degree or another, is oriented toward changing the person's world view and enhancing his awareness of options and resources (Bandler & Grinder, 1975).

In order to change a person's basic identity structure, the dynamics of his relationship to his family of origin must be addressed and altered. Such an intervention includes the need to explore his internalization or introjection of family issues as well as his current relationships with family members.

There are many treatment approaches such a process can take (Satir & Baldwin, 1983; Nerin, 1986; Bowen, 1972; Boszormenyi-Nagy & Spark, 1973; Williamson, 1978). Even those models of intervention which do not overtly ascribe to a method of resolution of family of origin issues (Haley, 1973; Minuchin, 1980; Erickson, 1977) have developed methods of altering the family systems' negative or ineffectual information, familial patterns and reinforcement. Behavior modification, far removed from a family systems approach, for example, focuses on changing behavior patterns formed or reinforced by the client's environment, i.e., family. Can one imagine the conduct of any type of therapy which would never include the words, for the patient or therapist, "mother" or "father?" Likewise the words "husband," "wife" and "child" are also central.

FAMILY OF PROCREATION: UNIT OF HEALING

Together with the family of origin, a therapist is ordinarily a member of a marital relationship, with or without children, or some alternative form of a significant relationship. This family unit is defined as the family of procreation, and in contrast to the biological family, has the possibility, and certainly the hope, of becoming the *unit of healing*. Many traumatic events a person experienced in his family of origin may be resolved through the family of procreation.

Satir theorized that people approach their marriages with the "hope of a second chance" (1972a). She postulated that whatever disappointment, hurt, problems or deficits one experienced in his family of origin, a person will be looking consciously, and more importantly, unconsciously, for a mate to fulfill such empty dark holes. A marriage and children of one's own can often generate a healing experience no other life context can produce. By being in therapy with a person's spouse or children present, the current family has the possibility of developing a greater empathy and appreciation for one another.

Paradoxically, the same dynamic of the hope for a second chance can be, and often is, the source of marital dysfunction and finally of marital rupture and divorce. By attempting to have one's family of procreation heal the wounds and scars of the past, especially with a chaotic family of origin history, the marital relationship frequently cannot stand the weight, and the relationship can become dysfunctional and disintegrate.

Out of this paradox, however, is another key to the resolution of family issues: the complementary nature of the families of origin and procreation leads to the interchangeability of healing and identity within the therapeutic context. Thus, a therapist can frequently use the family of origin as the source of healing for a marital dysfunction or loss. A judicious marital therapy can utilize interventions in both the families of origin and procreation to address not only issues within the marriage, but also to focus on unresolved issues and identify confusion from the client's original family system. Murray Bowen treats couples by focusing on each spouse's unresolved issues with their families of origin and purposefully defocuses attention on the marital or current family dynamics (1978).

Therefore, both past and present family structures can be an essential resource and fertilizer for individual healing and the development of a solid self. Expert therapists learn how to assess the strengths and problems of each family unit and how to frame their interventions accordingly. The ability to evaluate and utilize both family structures with ease is an invaluable therapeutic tool for the clinician.

To illustrate the integral connection between the therapist's clinical work with both his family of origin and his family of procreation, a series of transcripts follows which depicts one therapist's clinical and personal dilemmas. The work with this therapist was selected because it offered an opportunity to witness the variety of issues within both family units, and the subsequent effect on the therapist's thinking, acting and relating to clients he was treating. The transcripts provide a platform to examine, in depth, one therapist's struggle to identify and define himself as well as attempt to significantly improve his clinical performance.

TRAINING FOR THE PERSON AND PRACTICE OF THE THERAPIST

Transcripts

A member of a clinical training program, "The Person and Practice of the Therapist," conducted at the Family Institute of Virginia, participated over a nine-month training period in a variety of clinical and personal development efforts. In addition to each specific presentation, a holistic picture of the trainee, including his personal and clinical strengths and limitations, emerged. The following transcripts represent a variety of interventions utilized in the *Person/Practice* model. Besides the modalities and specific interventions transcribed, the therapist also wrote a conceptual description, prior to each presentation, evaluating his selected issue (clinical or self).

Since the *Person/Practice* model of training focuses on both the clinical competence and personal development of the practitioner, each trainee independently selects an area of skill development to focus upon during his presentation. Thus, a sphere of external and internal skill development of this particular therapist is presented, according to the selections he made.

The therapist, Jay, was a first-year member of the clinical training program. He was an alcoholism counselor and a recovering alcoholic. He was 41 years old, married for a second time with a 13-year-old daughter from his first marriage whom he saw on "visiting weekends."

Included are transcripts of the four times he presented in the training program during the nine months. In each instance there were two leaders, W and A, and 12 trainee participants. One additional transcript depicts a session when Jay came with his wife to be interviewed by their therapist. This interview took place in a separate clinical training program in which their therapist participated. Their marital therapist had requested that Jay and his wife come for a live interview as a consultation for herself with the trainers, W and A. Thus, Jay's own colleagues in training with him did not witness his live marital interview.

In Jay's first presentation, he reported on his work with a family, in the second he chose to present his own family history, and in the third he discussed his relationship with an alcoholic patient. In the fourth, he conducted a live session with the family that he discussed in his first case consultation at the beginning of the year. The session in which he and his wife were interviewed by their therapist occurred between Jay's first and second clinical presentations.

Throughout the training process, Jay was assisted in identifying a primary theme that emerged in both his clinical work and in his personal life: his fear and anticipation of rejection and subsequent defensive response of withdrawal in anger. The training efforts with him centered on helping him to become disposed toward making changes in these patterns. The focus of change was directed toward: his assuming a different perspective on his family of origin, including both past and present experiences with them; his connecting with family members and realigning his relationships with them; his attempting to make an adjustment in his approach toward his marriage and in his participation in marital therapy; and, most critically, toward his ameliorating clinical deficits and blind spots, particularly as they applied to the cases he presented; and finally, his identifying and learning to use his clinical resources, assets and personal style.

First Presentation

In Jay's first presentation he described a nuclear family with two parents, a son of 17 and a daughter of 16. His written description of the case concentrated on the father's ambition for his son and the young man's recent decline in school performance and his use of marijuana and alcohol. In the ensuing discussion with the leaders, it was revealed that the boy had recently impregnated the girl he was dating. Only the father and not the mother nor sister was aware of this fact. Jay's prior work with the family had focused on what he saw as the young man's rebellion against his father's overinvolvement with him. Jay's therapeutic approach primarily reflected his perception of the controlling and destructive aspects of the father's relationship with his son. This view limited his therapeutic interventions to helping the boy distance further from his father and to blocking the father's moves toward his son. There was relatively little focus on the mother or sister as evidenced by the fact that the therapist had colluded with the father and son to prevent the mother from knowing that her son had gotten his girlfriend pregnant.

The following is an excerpt from Jay's dialogue with the two leaders. It starts with one of the leaders saying to Jay that perhaps he does not recognize the genuine emotion between father and son.

A: You don't address, you don't acknowledge that at all.
Jay: And there is an affection.
A: It's like the father's hangup, that he has this thing about his son.
W: He's "narcissistic."
A: Right. Not that this father may love his son, however imperfect this father is, and that the son, no matter how imperfect he is, that the son loves his father and wants his father's love.
Jay: Yes.
A: You don't address that. You don't acknowledge it . . .
Jay: Right.
A: You move towards separating them in the way you write this up. What appears here is a young man who created his own separation from his father and very possibly the way he separated from his father led him to tearing himself down.
W: "Making poor grades on his SATs. Starting to smoke dope." My question is, "How do you make sense. . . . How does this relate to you?"
Jay: Well, I think what I saw was a distance from my father. What you said earlier struck me because I would notice that, but I wouldn't give that prime attention because my father and I weren't close at all. This is

just foreign territory for me. It's like a blind start. I can see the usage of control and freedom and power struggles, that I can relate to because I am familiar with that personally, but in terms of . . .

A: The core of feel of the love.

Jay: Yes, I just don't feel. There's a void in me there.

W: It has to do with bonding and affection.

At this point the leaders sought *a link* between Jay's clinical approach and his personal self. In response, Jay revealed the theme, "because my father died . . . I got dramatically cut off. It's like there has been a sense of insecurity about me . . ." As a result of this presentation, a picture of the therapist emerged which illuminated a man who cared deeply about his clients; wanted to resolve father-son disagreements and distance, both the client's as well as his own; had difficulty including women in his interventions and focus of change; and blocked out the emotional needs and bonds of client families as well as his own. Jay, like most other therapists, struggles with the universal problem of clinical blind spots and personal flaws.

Second Interview

Two months after his first case presentation, Jay came with his wife, Penny, who is also a recovered alcoholic, to meet with G, their marital therapist. This live interview was viewed by the same trainers and their therapists' own training group through an observation mirror. G first met with the leaders and her own training group to discuss her work with Jay and Penny. She reported that Jay had recently made a shift in his relationship with her which she believed may have been in response to his first presentation in his group.

G: He came in for the last session. He requested a session alone because he has not been doing very well. It was the first time he really opened up to me. He said, "I know I'm very guarded, that I'm very guarded with you." That's when I brought up doing this thing (the live observed session). This has only begun to change in the last month since he's been in the training group. And I hold back from him. I can feel it. I'm not, I just stay away.

She further added:

He's easy to get in an argument with and I'm not always successful at, oh. . . . He has been very defensive with me. When I say anything to him that is at all critical, he gets very defensive. Right away. So I tread softly. When I get into it with him, it's real unhelpful. He's real oppositional. I just feel like I don't want to sit there and convince him he should be in therapy, he should work on his marriage, that he should do anything.

In the family session (with therapist, Jay and Penny):

G: . . . What is it going to take for you, Jay, to sit down with Penny and be able to talk to her about feeling defensive?

Jay: . . . I withdrew. I became detached, which is my system anyway, as you well know. I'm very good at that. I've been doing that ever since I was about five years old. If I perceive that I'm not getting through or if I was to say something and it didn't have a positive effect, I would withdraw and go off and do something else and I kind of detach from her. So we wind up in different sections of the house. (To Penny) Either I'm in the den and you're in the bedroom or I'm in the bedroom and you're in the den watching TV. Doing our little thing. It's kind of like two people living under the same roof, but really not interacting.

Shortly afterwards, Penny and Jay interchange:

Penny: To be honest, Jay, I don't really understand what some of your anxieties are. I don't know exactly where you are coming from there. You know, whether you feel that. . . . I think maybe one of them is the fact that you don't think I really care about you, that I really love you. That I don't respect you. And I think. . . . Well, you did say, "I don't honestly think you care one way or the other about me."

G: Jay?

Jay: Well, I think that's true. At times I doubt, I vacillate. Some days I think that you do and other days I'm not sure if you do. I have some fears . . . that you want to control. I'm just afraid of that. That's something that scares me. I mean, that doesn't pertain to anything we've done in the marriage, that was, you know, that way before. But it is still a concern I have that that would happen. That I'd be used.

Later in the session:

G: In order to come out, you are going to need to feel security from this guy. Just talk to him about feeling threatened. Don't go off on your . . .

Penny: (To Jay) I really don't feel secure with you. I know this is very painful and it's very painful for me to say it. I don't feel I can lean on you. I don't really feel that, if push came to shove, that you'd be there for me. I don't really feel cheerful with anyone and in any way. I don't know how to spell it out. I feel like I'm pretty much on my own and I've felt that way since after the third month we were married. Therefore, it's very hard to tell you what my real needs are and yet you talk about telling me your anxieties and that it would upset me . . .

With G's encouragement, Jay crawls further out on the limb for Penny.

Jay: Well, I want to say that I am sorry that I wasn't able to be of more support for you and identify with your pain more than I was able to do. I think you are right. I did have a hard time with that. It isn't that I don't know that you are hurting, and it isn't that I don't want to help you. I think that your hurt and depression really overwhelmed me, too. It scared me and I didn't know what to do.

I do care about you a lot and I don't want you to be where you're at with yourself. I get impatient. That's one of my defects of character. When I say something and you don't understand it, then I get frustrated and angry at you or I'll detach and that's something that I need to not do anymore . . .

Here is the pattern Jay has of keeping distance, wanting intimacy, but not risking himself to get involved with his wife while maintaining a self. Whenever the inevitable conflict that arises from their differences surfaces, his solution (which was illustrated earlier, in his clinical case) is to withdraw, avoid and, eventually, feel angry and let down by his wife. This pattern is a replication of the relational structure from his family of origin. Jay's ties to his father were severed by death, and he eventually cut himself off from his mother and sister. However, with his therapist's encouragement, he reached out for his wife, and this relationship became a model, or parallel process, for extending himself to his clients.

Third Presentation

In Jay's next presentation in his training group, he chose to explore in depth the dynamics of his family of origin. The themes of distance, fear and self-esteem again emerged. His father, who had been an alcoholic, died in an automobile accident when Jay was seventeen. Here he is talking with the leaders, W and A.

A: Yes. It makes a lot of sense. Did your father love you?
Jay: I don't know.
W: What do you know about your love for him?
Jay: Well, I know I wanted his approval. I always felt good when he gave me some attention. But he was gone a lot, he worked seven days a week, 12 hours a day occasionally. When I was young, he wasn't around that much.
W: What did he do for a living?
Jay: He was a veterinarian, but not a present type. We lived out in the country. He did a lot of heavy work. . . . Big farm animals. Huge animals and a lot of them. So, sometimes he would take me along, but usually he didn't because usually he would be gone for such a long period of time that it wouldn't have been appropriate. So, he wasn't around a lot. When he was, he was frequently drunk. It's pretty hard to relate to now. He was very angry. I always thought he was a lot angrier at my mother than he was at me, but sometimes I caught it anyway. So I learned to retreat and go out and escape from potentially violent situations. . . . Their (his parents) relationship was awful. It was just terrible.

* * *

Yes. I knew that when I was young. It never got any better, never. Even when he stopped drinking so much. I mean, the violent arguments stopped, but the tension was incredible. You could cut it with a knife. It was really a classic case of that. So, I got the hell out of there as much as I could without abandoning my responsibilities to the family, especially my mother who I did feel protective towards.

* * *

Jay: I know that he was angry with my mother because of the fact that she was closer to me than he was.

A: That you didn't care about your father.

W: Or that she never let him get close to you. She may have needed you all for herself and wouldn't share you.

Jay: Yes, that's true. She made that quite clear. So, I took her side when I was young because my father, he wasn't around to defend himself. When he was around, he was drinking. It did seem like she was getting the shaft. As I got older, though, I began to see the situation a little differently. It wasn't quite as one-sided. Then I felt betrayed by my mother because I said, "Wait a minute now."

W: Then he died.

Jay: Then he died. Right.

W: What do you feel about your father from the other people who he nursed there, from some of the people he served? Do you know anything about how he was seen, how he was perceived, what he did for them?

Jay: No, I don't know much about his work at all. He had a few friends in town who would get together once in a while and play bridge. That was the extent of his social life.

W: But you don't know anything about how these other people felt about having a sick animal that they needed something done for and he fixed it for them?

Jay: No, I know nothing about that.

W: And what happened . . . ?

Jay: Excuse me?

W: What feelings are you aware of as I bring that up now?

Jay: Well, I was proud of him for the work he did because he worked hard and did a good job.

W: Do you know how long it took in this meeting for you to say that?

Jay: There's kind of an emptiness because I don't know a lot about him. I know some things about him, but I really don't know him. I wish I knew more about him, but I don't. What he was really feeling and what people said to him and the things that happened in his life. I just really don't know.

W: nd how he was viewed in the community.

Jay: I remember just before he died, he was elected to the town council.

A: He certainly wasn't the village drunk, right?

Jay: No. No, he wasn't the village drunk. . . . I was surprised when he ran for office. I couldn't believe it. What the hell is going on here? Because it seemed so unlike him to become involved in community activities. Up until that point in time I had always seen him as an isolated man, a private person. So, I was really surprised. I was really proud of him when he ran for office. I said, "Boy, that's great." But again, I don't know what he did. I never went to any meetings. Again, I felt excluded from all that.

A: But you do know that there is a bond between you and your father. You've described it here. Look at this tape afterwards.

Jay: When I was growing up, my mother and I were very close, the outline indicates. I think we felt, I felt, threatened because my father had a severe drinking problem. But, in spite of that, I know at a very young age that my mother would make statements about people that did not seem to be true. She would talk about the neighbors plotting against us, and it seemed to me that it didn't make sense because my father would get along fine with these people. We'd be out in the yard raking leaves and he'd be talking to Mr. Broder and Mrs. Boss, Mr. Boss, Mr. Hanson. They were just ordinary folks, but my mother would say, "Well, they don't like us." If a bush in our yard was damaged or a limb was broken off a tree, my mother would say, "Well, someone came over and broke it off the tree." Now, even at a young age, I had a feeling that something was wrong because I didn't believe that. I didn't believe that Mr. Boss was going to come over and break a limb off our tree. It just didn't make any sense. I laugh, but it's sad. I figured if somebody did that, my dad would have done something, and he didn't seem to be doing anything about it, these occurrences. So, then it was likely my mother didn't love me, and father doesn't love me, and my sister hates me.

* * *

. . . It didn't make any sense to me. When I saw those people. . . . I have to admit that my grandmother was a little bit out in left field.

W: What do you mean?

Jay: She was a little bit nuts. I think she was a little, well, in retrospect, manic depressive and at times, violent. In fact, at the age of sixty, she assaulted me one morning in the kitchen of our house.

W: Just started beating up on you?

Jay: Yes. I was cooking bacon and eggs, and I turned around and, suddenly, there was a left hook in my jaw and I went reeling across the kitchen, came back and took one in the nose, a right cross. Here's my grandmother. So, my instinct was to flatten her, but I said to myself, "No. She's sixty years old. You can't." So, I went up and immobilized her. Her eyes were flashing.

* * *

W: How old were you then?

Jay: Nineteen.

W: So, you do know something about your mother's parents and what happened to her. More than you realize you know. So, she had a manic depressive mother which would make you a little paranoid if you were a child. Especially in that era. Think about it, when was your grandmother born?

Jay: 1899.

W: There was no lithium then.

Jay: No, there wasn't.

W: Have you ever thought about that before? About what it would be like for your mother to have a manic depressive mother? Who could be unpredictably violent?

Jay: No. I'm saying manic depressive just by, uh. . . . I know my grandmother talked to herself a lot when we were at the house and seemed to not be always with what we were talking about—off in her own world. She would get to storming around the house. She would pick up knives and wave them. Then other times, she was extremely friendly and laughable and nice. A real charming, brilliant, talented woman. Heavy set, looks like a manic depressive. Really has the look. But she'd get wild and not sleepy and stay up all hours of the night. So, I don't know. What was the impact of that on my mother? I don't know that I've ever really thought about it very much.

* * *

W: When your father died, how did your mother change toward you?

Jay: Well, there was like an immediate distancing. I mean, like it was just very dramatic. Her focus shifted. It had, we had been pulling apart anyway a little bit, but, you know, I was okay because I was just growing older. We were still friendly. It was substantially normal, I guess you could say. But suddenly it was like I couldn't talk to her anymore. She just pulled back from me. It is hard to describe. She didn't seem to want to deal with anything that I had to say about anything.

* * *

W: How did you feel? How were you affected by that change in her? Jay: It drove me crazy. I just. . . . I felt separated from her like I was traumatically separated. Like suddenly, I didn't understand her anymore. The person who I had gotten used to relating to . . . suddenly I couldn't relate to anymore. I felt distant. I was confused because I didn't know why. I didn't understand what was happening. I was overwhelmed. I was hurt. Then suddenly, I wasn't hurt. It was like I wasn't her son anymore and it was like she just wanted me to leave. That's the way I felt. Just get out.

W: What do you think that was all about? How do you make sense of it? I know you see everything as related to you, but try to think of it in a larger context.

Jay: . . . I just don't know. I've never been able to figure the damage here. I know she seemed to turn inward and also my sister. Since I had a very close relationship with my sister, that's what infuriated . . . because all of a sudden, I was being blocked there. I was just clearly being undermined. I was really angry with my sister 'cause she was "letting it happen." I was losing my influence I had always had – the big brother influence.

* * *

Yes. Emotionally to me. All I had was my dog. Then my dog died a year later. I remember going into mourning. I cried all night long. That was the end, you know. That was the last thing, the last love relationship that I really had and I just lost that. . . . I went to pieces, just absolutely to pieces. I was always trying to figure out that reaction and it's becoming clear to me this morning. So, my sister said, "Well, you're not it." Then my mother said, "You're not it. You're not only not her father, you're not my son," in a sense.

* * *

A: And to this woman, having somebody take care of her was the single most important need of her life. Somebody she could rely on. Somebody that could belong to her so she wouldn't be alone in her paranoia. So, there could at least be her and your sister against the world instead of her being against the world all alone. It's a very desperate woman, a very frightened woman, a very vulnerable woman.

W: And you fulfilled her fears.

Jay: Well, that makes a lot of sense to me. I mean, I see that and I really appreciate your helping to put some words where there have been only feelings. I just, . . . even though I've had a lot of pity for her, I've also really hated her because she did use my sister for that when my sister was nine years old and vulnerable. So, I think that if I'm around my mother, what I feel is just this overwhelming hatred. I don't think it has as much to do with her relationship with me as it does with her relationship with Sandra. At least that is what I prefer to believe. My real hate comes from . . . I don't know.

* * *

Jay: I just can't understand how I can look at other people's families and see what's going on when I look at myself and I can't understand anything . . .

At this point, Jay had only seen his mother once in eleven years. He had little to do with his sister except for some correspondence. However, his sister had recently responded to a small overture on his part (initiated after he joined the training group) and was considering a visit with her brother. He was encouraged to come to terms with his mother as he tried to renew his relationship with his sister, so that he would not enter a repeat competition with his mother for his sister.

Jay was beginning to see the connection between how the rejection he had experienced in his life had precipitated a cut-off, withdrawal and anger toward his mother and sister as well as everyone else in his family of origin. His continued pattern of withdrawal from the significant figures in his early life was also binding him to his personal contributions to the distance and anger between himself and his wife, and to issues of personal vulnerability and intimacy in the families he treated, as well as in his therapeutic relationships with his clients.

After these presentations (clinical, family of procreation and family of origin), the linkages between the three arenas become apparent. The connection between Jay's feelings about his mother and his wife were clarified when he stated to his wife,

> . . . I am sorry that I wasn't able to be more support for you and identify with your pain. . . . I did have a hard time with that. . . . That your hurt and depression really overwhelmed me, too. It scared me and I didn't know what to do.

Clearly, Jay hoped that his marriage could be a unit of healing for the wounds he sustained in his own family of origin, or unit of identity. When the marital dynamics replicated his original struggles and formation of family of origin cut-offs, he isolated himself from his wife, just as he had learned to do with his mother.

The training effort with him aimed at helping him to understand these connections, to begin finding ways to do something about his family life, and translating these changes into more useful therapeutic relationships and effective clinical interventions with families.

Fourth Presentation

In his fourth presentation, Jay talked about the struggle he was experiencing in a relationship with a client. It became apparent that this client who, like Jay, is a recovering alcoholic, paralleled some of Jay's patterns with close relationships. Jay had been the counselor who had been most significant in helping this client become sober. He had become one of the very few people that his client had learned to trust and Jay had become attached to the client. However, in recent months, Jay had ceased functioning as his primary counselor, although he was still seeing the client in a group he was leading. Hypothetically, both client and therapist were experiencing the loss of their individual therapy relationship. However, Jay did not express an awareness of the loss. The client was reacting angrily, being difficult in the group, and unpredictable in the alcohol treatment program. Jay reported that he was frustrated with his client and no longer knew how to deal with him.

This excerpt begins with Jay revealing how he can become so angry with people who have been close to him and then let him down that he literally has murderous fantasies. (Interestingly, these feelings are quite similar to the response he had to his mother. By starting with a close, undifferentiated "we" relationship with his mother, feeling rejected and pushed away, he distanced to protect himself and ended with anger, or as Jay stated, with a feeling of " . . . if I'm around my mother, what I feel is this overwhelming hatred.")

Jay: . . . If someone really does commit to someone, gets close to somebody and then if you were to be let down, it really does hurt. It hurts me so much that I get ready to kill them or maim them and that's pretty scary. . . . I don't want to kill anybody, especially clients. . . .

Jay had seen action in Vietnam. A member of the training group, who was also a veteran, spontaneously volunteered some support to Jay based on the bonds of their friendship and a conversation they had the night before at a get-together of the trainees. Apparently, they were talking about Jay's experience of killing in battle. The trainee's comments follow the leader's allusion to Jay's anger toward his own father. Jay felt his father did not appreciate him, which was also how he described his client's attitude toward him.

Trainee: There is another time when it's (anger) appropriate, too. If you live through it, when somebody shoots at you, that's the ultimate rejection. If you get mad enough to shoot back hard so they don't shoot back at you anymore, then you are safe.

Jay: I know that. I understand that. Killing for me is a definite option, emotionally.

Trainee: You've done it. You know you've done it. You talked about dealing with the rage and anger last night. . . . So, you have so much experience that you put a lid on, that it comes out with this guy. It comes out with the talking about your family. I mean you have had experiences that not everybody has.

Jay: Yes. You're right. I thank you a lot. Thanks for telling me that.

Trainee: Everybody that you know you kill, even though you love them if you start to think of them as husbands, fathers.

W: I really appreciate what you just did, Brett, and it makes me aware how important it is for there to be a group and how important it is for you all to have time (outside the formal program time) when you can just let down your hair and be in a context where you can socialize together and get into conversations of this kind . . .

Jay: (Talking a little later about his closeness to clients) . . . They express my pain for me, and I feel that's a fair trade because I help them.

(Qualifying his comments about his current perspective toward his father and about his changing attitude toward his mother) . . . I noticed what I felt as a significant change from the time two months ago . . . it is the way I felt about my Dad. It seems to have impacted the way I feel about myself. I am going to try to use this today. I don't think that I've been very sensitive to my mother's situation and I think I've hurt myself by not being sensitive to what was happening to her. I'm going to try to deal with that somehow and understand it better. I will talk to my aunt (from whom he had also cut off). I'm also probably not very sensitive to my wife's situation.

Yes. And this particular guy, I think there is something here because . . . you know, all of the clients I've dealt with . . . with whom I have felt totally inadequate . . . this one guy is right at the top of that list . . . it's been bothering me a lot. I can't figure out why I've lost my perspective on the guy . . .

And I think he attaches some of that (his recovery) to me. That I'm part of the successful episode in his life, and he has always looked upon me as being very special. We have maintained contact off and on through the last two and a half years. He called me and asked to join my group. He trusts me probably as much as he trusts anybody.

W: So, do you see him as in a transference relationship with you?

After uncovering the source of Jay's problems, the client's identification with Jay and their respective reactions to one another, the trainers refocused their intervention on the resolution of Jay's technical problems with the case.

A: (Asking Jay how he has been responding to his client's angry behavior in the alcohol therapy group) Yes. I don't know whether you just stayed quiet, whether you ignored what he said, whether every time he accuses you of something, if you turned to everybody else and said, "Is he right? Back me. Protect me against him."

Jay: Yes, that's what I did.

* * *

I would be very angry. I would be expressing . . .

A: Spell it out.

Jay: Just an enormous degree of frustration over Bill's (his client) willingness to use what is being said to help himself. Just my own pain over being . . .

W: Over being . . .

Jay: Not being . . . just being misperceived and not being appreciated. Not being appreciated for the amount of effort and concern that I really do have for this guy. That's . . .

W: Can you say any more about the tender feeling you have for him?

Jay: You've got me there. I'm seeing something – that I haven't been honest with him.

W: About your tenderness?

Jay: Yes.

W: Will you be honest with us?

Jay: I really like Bill, and I care about him and I appreciate him a lot. I have a lot of respect for him, and I have a lot of sympathy and compassion for Bill. He touches me. I know what he has been through. He's done a lot, I think, in the face of really heavy odds. I feel real close to him in that regard. I identify with him very much there and I suppose that, in a sense, there is a kind of brotherly feeling that I have for him. And so when he began to reject me, I just couldn't deal with it.

A: He betrayed you.

Jay: Yes, he betrayed me.

A: What is it that you didn't tell him?

Jay: I didn't tell him any of this. I didn't even see it. I just didn't see it. I don't know why. It's like I'm blind to my own transference. Shit. (Sighs.)

Jay finished the interview planning how he would deal with his client about their relationship, reinforcing and connecting this action with his intention to also deal with his mother, sister, and aunt.

Fifth Presentation

For Jay's final presentation, he brought in the family that he had described in his first clinical consultation for a live interview. In the following excerpt, one sees Jay pursuing the parents, but particularly, the father (with whom he privately identifies) to reduce the emotional barriers between the father and his adolescent son and daughter.

Jay: (Addressing the father) That's what you could talk to him (the son) about. What do you need from her (daughter)?

Father: To know what's going on.

Jay: Anything else?

Father: Well, we're obviously. . . . I need to be loved by her, you know, yes, that's obvious, and it should not go unstated and that's true with Cal (son) and that's true with my wife.

Jay: Does that get stated very much?

Father: That doesn't get stated very much.

Jay: Well, it's important as issues go. (Turning to wife) Do you share your husband's feelings?

Mother: Yes, we do.

Jay: What could be done?

Daughter: Loosen up. Don't be afraid to say it.
Jay: Don't be afraid to say, "I love you."
Mother: Or write it. It's nice to hear it from kids, too, not just parents telling kids.
Jay: Well, you would like them to say it?
Mother: Of course.
Father: I want Cal to talk about his actions yesterday.
Son: You know about it already.

There is an interruption from a telephone call by the trainers. At this point, the father was distracting the conversation from his need for his children's love to inquire about some minor trouble his son got into the day before. The father's diversion began to distance him from his children. The trainers knew Jay was vulnerable to being reinducted into his disposition to defend himself against closeness. Therefore, they suggested to Jay that he keep the focus on the emotional issues between the father and his children.

Jay: You know this thing about love. (Unclear phrase.) It is so important to be able to show it. Communicate it (soft voice, unclear phrase). (Turning to daughter) How did you feel when your dad said he needed some love?
Daughter: (Long pause) I mean I know that. I need that.
Jay: Is it hard for you to tell him that you love him? Why so quiet? If we're quiet we all die. We need love and it's changed everybody's behavior. It's like we're all solemn now. Oh, God, we're talking about love! Because where there isn't that communication of love (unclear phrase) because we need it so much.

. . . But what we're talking about here is intimacy. It's just sharing each other's time and souls without regard to rules or success or failure. It's just sharing some time to get to know each other.

At this point, all family members are tearful.

. . . In a sense we are talking about barriers. We could spend time trying to identify barriers and patterns, but to kind of achieve a sense of closure, I want to agree with you and I think the issue here is unconditional love. . . . I think

> that's really what you need to do more than anything else. To spend some time getting to know each other. I guess I've always really wanted to say that, and I don't really know why I haven't, but the unconditional love just really . . . it does ring true to me. I see you suffering.

Jay came around the full circle, interviewing the family he first talked about when he entered the clinical training program. The therapist had begun with discussing his efforts to create distance between a father and son in a family he was treating; engaged in a consultation about his dysfunctional marital relationship; progressed on to explore the issues and emotional cut-off in his own family of origin; then moved to his stuck, angry relationship with a client who was important to him; and ended with an effort to generate emotional bonds between family members that paralleled the change Jay had begun in his own life. Jay took steps to resolve the issues around his cut-off from his family of origin by seeing his father as a more caring and worthwhile person, initiating a process to reconnect with his mother and sister with whom he had developed more empathy. With his therapist's help, he also took steps to risk more of himself to get closer to his wife, who was fearful of bonding with her husband. Jay's efforts lowered the barrier he had erected to intimacy with all the subsequent risks and disappointment inherent in such a change. This work also provided him with maps for how to resolve a conflictual father and son relationship. Similarly, Jay learned to reach out to a client whom he felt had spurned their therapeutic relationship.

IMPLICATIONS FOR THE THERAPIST

Every therapist, like Jay, has a personal history, deeply rooted in his family life. A therapist's life is an intricate, one of a kind, tapestry. There is a "passion novel" to be explored with a primary plot structure as well as secondary themes. When a practitioner understands himself as a person and the effect of his individual history on his identity, he greatly enhances his ability to master himself (*internal* or personal skills) in the process of conducting successful therapy (*external* or technical skills), as well as learn new theoretical material (Aponte & Winter, 1987).

An important initial step toward this goal is the *identification of themes in his life history*. A therapist's experiences with his family of origin and family of procreation thus become one of his primary textbooks. The material contained in that epistle will frequently shed light onto his clinical dilemmas where theory or technique cannot help him move toward change or resolution with a client.

A therapist needs to learn within his own family context: what has and is happening; how he characteristically tends to handle issues within the therapeutic relationship as a result of experiences with his family; what types of clients does he identify with or distance from; what unresolved or perhaps even unresolvable issues exist within himself and his family; how to utilize his own victories and defeats to effectively engage with clients; and how to discern and develop a process to manage his therapeutic behavior for the benefit of the client's change.

By identifying and understanding such issues, a therapist can not only benefit his clients, but paradoxically, as Kaslow asserted, "Clearly, then, not only does a therapist's family life affect his training and practice, but his professional development has interpersonal ramifications for his family life" (1984a, p. 86).

RESOLUTION OF THE PSYCHOTHERAPIST'S FAMILY ISSUES

Implicitly, there is reciprocity between a practitioner's clinical performance and his unresolved family patterns (Satir, 1986; Bowen, 1972, 1978; Freud, 1957). Likewise, there is a correlation between a person's past and present world view (Watzlawick, 1984) where each temporal orientation continuously impacts upon and influences the other.

Consequently, a therapist undertakes the process of identifying personal themes and moving toward family resolution in order to improve his present functioning, both as a clinician and as a person. Such effort simultaneously addresses the interchangeability of the personal and professional domains of a practitioner's life. Disentanglement from one's past allows the person of the therapist to no longer be a prisoner of the past; rather, it changes his focus toward developing his full clinical potential in the present.

Solving personal family dilemmas for a clinician does not necessarily mean "and they lived happily ever after." Resolution has a wide range of meaning which can lead a person to a number of possible choices. Technically, resolution means to: break up into separate parts; change or transform; find a solution or an answer; explain or make clear; or make a decision about. Many fields utilize the concept of resolution. In music it is the passing of a dissonant chord to a consonant chord. Optics defines resolution as the capability of a system to make clear and distinguishable the separate parts or components of an object, or of differentiating between sources of light. In medicine it is defined as a subsistence or disappearance of swelling, fever or other manifestation of a disease. Finally, literature employs resolution as part of a drama or narrative in which the plot is unraveled.

From a family systems perspective, every definition above provides a choice for the person to consider and employ. Past events cannot change, yet one's perception and understanding, in the present, can transform a person's responses. One's current relationships or disposition toward persons associated with the past can change. Family resolution, in essence, is working out a state of mind through a relational context. The Alcoholic's Anonymous "Prayer of Serenity" can serve as a guideline for the person of the therapist endeavoring to unscramble his past as well as help client families do the same: "God grant me the serenity to accept the things I cannot change, courage to change the things I can and wisdom to know the difference." By accepting, reinterpreting and changing how one deals with old events, patterns and people, the therapist gains new potential in his therapeutic skills.

Just as there are "many roads to Rome," so, too, has the field of family systems developed a number of models for resolution of a therapist's family issues, including:

- Bowen's method of "coaching" a therapist to individually deal with his own parents and develop a "personal relationship" with each family member while maintaining a sense of his own unique self (1972).
- Kaslow's family and marital psychotherapy process which utilizes a "diaclectic" psychodynamic and systems approach toward family change, thus enabling therapists "to be able to risk establishing intense therapeutic alliances, when appropriate" (1984a, p. 86).
- Satir's Family Reconstruction process which is an enactment procedure focusing on key nodal events in the family's life. It aims at changing the identity structure and early life trance states or "old learnings." This method is particularly useful, for example, when a therapist does not have access to his family members as a result of death (Nerin, 1986; Satir & Baldwin, 1983).
- Williamson's approach, described as developing "new life at the graveyard" (1978).
- Other methods designed to alter or change the therapist's unit of identity, including: letter writing; talking to family friends; ancestral homages; and Gestalt therapy.

Regardless of the model utilized to develop family resolution, there are a variety of components which provide choices for each individual to approach his family. One major stumbling block for dissolving family problems is a therapist's reluctance to give up the known, with its "old shoe comfortableness," and move on toward the unknown, with its attendant strangeness and unfamiliarity (Satir, 1982). By breaking down this immense, lifelong task into understandable and elemental steps, a therapist can more easily imagine himself engaging in a process of family resolution. Such imagery can lessen his anxiety and fear. Changing one's identity structure as well as the homeostasis of his current family life requires a skillful intervention process.

The following represents a sampling of components which may be utilized in family resolution:

- Coming to understand how systems work, including power, boundary, alignment, hierarchy, scapegoating, projection process, equilibrating forces, etc. gives the therapist: an intellectual and universal view of family systems; an idea that he is not alone in the struggle; and, a conceptual map of theoretical change.
- Finding out the social ecology of each parent's own family allows the therapist to know what external forces impacted upon the total family system. Such discoveries help the person to develop a world context and, subsequently, create a frame of reference for family events, decision-making and values. Learning the ecological context can assist the clinician to depersonalize what frequently may be highly charged, emotional events by assisting him in his process observations and consequent independence.
- Discovering the process and facts surrounding family events aids the therapist in developing an internal coherence with regard to his family's life. For example, if a person realizes that his parents lost five children prior to his birth, their overprotective involvement with him is less likely to be interpreted as a result of his own, or his parents', personal characteristics and flaws. Thus, within the family context, such formerly aberrant behavior begins to make sense. Even the most painful events, such as parent/child incest can be better understood and resolved once the family's internal process is known.
- Absorbing the facts, similarly, is a critical step in the family change process. Facts can often lead to empathy and understanding or, at least, to a change in perception. For example, as Jay absorbed his grandmother's manic depressive episodes, or absorbed what it meant for his father to be an elected city official

and a veterinarian in a rural setting, his view of his father as a "drunk" and his mother as untrustworthy, greatly diminished.

- Dealing with unresolved issues directly with family members, where possible, and handling the attendant conflict and enmeshment, creates a present day change within the person's family relationships. This joint family interaction can ameliorate existing intra-family response patterns.
- Changing one's pattern of interaction with family members alters the family's structure. When a therapist unilaterally and intentionally changes his posture within his own family system, he modifies family organization in relation to himself. This approach is particularly useful when the family will not deal directly with him about unresolved family issues.
- Coming to see one's parents as human beings, instead of the idealized role of "mother" or "father," allows the practitioner to accept his own frailties and learn to cope with and manage his inevitable flaws. This process facilitates the forgiveness of self and parents for mistakes.
- Realizing what parents cannot change, letting go of the childhood wish to be taken care of, and determining that one can be self-sufficient, frees the therapist to be more autonomous.
- Negotiating an appropriate adult relationship with one's family further underscores the individual's self-esteem and differentiation. *Knowing that one can trust himself not to betray himself for love is a liberating, life sustaining event, as opposed to the quixotic pursuit of fully achieving family approval and acceptance.* In essence, this process aims to maintain self while in contact with significant others.

By transforming oneself with regard to family entanglements, changing the family interaction pattern, understanding and accepting the past, as well as altering his perception of the past, a therapist is more able to learn from and interact with people in his present and future life, including his own family and clinical cases. Regardless of the road traveled toward family resolution, as Kaslow cogently stated, the guiding principle of Boszormenyi-Nagy and Spark (1973) underpins such efforts:

> Through all of the reawakening and re-experiencing of our personal historic past, we are often guided to become aware of the "invisible loyalties" to significant biological relatives, particularly our parents, and to be mindful of the ethical-existential obli-

> gations that accrue by virtue of their having endowed us with the gift of life and, it is to be hoped, of love. (1984, p. 92)

Whatever model of intervention, the family of origin, with its ultimate gift of life, is the creator of identity, and establishes the formative patterns for one's personal relationships. A resolution of these core units must be addressed in order to develop autonomous, effective psychotherapists. Together with that, the family of procreation provides the foundation for a person's current social functioning and is a resource for healing old family wounds.

IMPLICATIONS FOR TREATMENT

Inherent in the *Person/Practice* model are a number of assumptions about the nature of treatment and the relationship between therapist and client. There are two primary domains of therapeutic skill development which converge regarding treatment assumptions. First, there are the *internal* or personal skills which represent "the personal integration of the therapist's own experiences and self in order to become a useful therapeutic instrument." Second, there are the *external* or technical skills which are the "actual technical behaviors utilized by the therapist in the conduct of therapy" (Aponte & Winter, 1987). Since the *Person/Practice* model holds that both forms of expertise are requisite for the therapist to achieve an excellent outcome for clients, the treatment implications of each domain will be addressed.

Internal or Personal Skills

Effective use of the person of the therapist is contingent upon the resolution of the clinician's personal and family issues, and his ability to manage within the therapeutic context those aspects of self that are flawed, incomplete, or unchangeable. To reiterate, three primary functions of a therapist's clinical performance are affected as a result of personal issues: thinking, relating and acting. The ability to conceptualize and see what is going on in a case, to develop relationships with family members, and to take appropriate action are involved in creating positive therapeutic outcomes.

It is also essential that the therapist assess each and every case he is treating for two areas of thematic identification – content themes and relational themes. Both dimensions can significantly affect the therapist's clinical performance.

First, *content themes* consist generally of topic areas, events, etc., which may trigger key memories or issues within the therapist. Every life carries a number of recurring and unifying subjects, like war, moves, ethnicity, death, divorce, illness, immigration, and special family relationships. As illustrated by Jay and his colleague in the training group, these two men had a strong identification through the theme of the Vietnam war, which became a moving and powerful event in Jay's presentation as it led him to feel safe and reveal more of his deeper, hidden drives. The next section on external skills provides explication on the use of content themes in the conduct of treatment.

Second, *relational themes* stem from a therapist's attributing to a client characteristics or likenesses which correctly belong to people within the therapist's own life. Freudians would term the process counter-transference. From a family systems perspective, Satir firmly asserts that whenever any three people are together the dynamics recreate the universal and basic triad of mother/father/child. Thus, she holds that a therapist must always be cognizant of what "hat" he is projecting onto each family member. She describes counter-transference as a "real case of mistaken identity" (1987, p. 6) and believes that since "therapy is a deeply intimate and vulnerable experience, requiring sensitivity to one's own state of being as well as to that of the other," treatment and healing cannot begin until such projected identities are shed, and there is "the meeting of the deepest self of the therapist with the deepest self of the patient or client" (1987, p. 1).

A necessary ingredient for the development of a therapist's projective process, however, is the element of similarity that a client or family system has with aspects of the clinician's own life. Such resemblances invariably elicit a projective dynamic from the therapist. From a systems perspective, there must be a component of reciprocity in the client which surfaces the therapist's identification and projective process. For example, it may be age, hair color, ethnicity, gender, or mannerisms. Thus, the projective process does not evolve solely from a therapist's own dynamics. It is generated by characteristics, values, and interactions of the client system as it meshes with the clinician's system.

The therapist's projective process originating from his identity developed through his family, personal experiences and current life situation leads him to form a pattern of relating to people and the world. Thus customary disposition of interacting becomes the basis for each therapist's *relational themes*. Thus, a woman who was "Daddy's Girl" will struggle in her therapy with men to utilize her power and leadership effectively rather than acting like a "coquette" to influence the outcome. Likewise, this same therapist will need to relate to the man's wife as a client rather than a competitor, which can be an outcome of a very close father/daughter relationship. Jay, for example, was cut off from both his father and mother through loss. Thus, he had developed a relational theme, a habitual disposition of relating, which was his distancing and noninvolvement with people. Although he is a sociable and pleasant man, as he stated to his wife, "I withdraw. I become detached, which is my system anyway. . . . I'm very good at that, I've been doing it since I was about five years old . . . "

Each therapist's projective process, and the context of his current life, solidifies into a recurrent pattern or disposition of interaction which forms his own relational themes. Especially in family therapy, a practitioner needs to acknowledge and master relational themes since the therapeutic process itself can literally enact and replicate aspects of his own family dynamics.

Another dimension in the use of self within the therapeutic context involves the clinician's development of autonomy and self-esteem. If the therapist is too dependent on the client to supply his or her sense of well-being and cannot handle the level of detachment necessary to help the client change, a successful treatment outcome is encumbered. A fundamental tenet of Bowen's is that a therapist's differentiation within his own family system is the essential component necessary to develop an autonomous, effective therapist. According to Bowen, "Everyone else is a piece of cake" after one has resolved the dynamics of their family of origin (Winter, 1986). Kaslow holds such a personal resolution allows the clinician to "risk establishing intense therapeutic alliances, when appropriate" (1984a, p. 4).

An underlying premise is that a therapist is ineffective if he needs a client's love and/or approval. A therapist must be able to endure the necessary personal distance and professional tension required to establish and maintain an effective therapeutic relationship. This is not to say that the client and therapist cannot be close. The key is that the therapist has a choice about the proximity of the therapeutic relationship and can alter his stances for the benefit of the client. This differentiation is a critical variable distinguishing between personal friendship and a therapeutic relationship.

Essentially, a therapist's competence depends not only upon his effective resolution of personal issues, but also on his ability to utilize within the therapeutic context what he has learned from the process of such resolutions. Also, a clinician's effectiveness is determined by his ability to manage within the therapeutic context his limitations, those aspects of his life and self that are still problematic.

External or Technical Skills

In addition to understanding and utilizing content and relational themes, a third clinical component impacts the therapeutic process. This integral part results from the combination of the therapist's personal characteristics transacting with the client's or family system's specific qualities. Each participant, in fact, brings his or her own individual content and relational themes as well as their respective personality structures, value systems, family relationships, career expertise, theoretical frameworks, world views, etc. Consequently, a new entity emerges which is the transactional context for change. This *therapeutic system* becomes the vehicle for personal change. It impacts all participants, including the therapist, and differs from case to case. Therefore, the practitioner enters into and creates a new therapeutic system in every clinical endeavor.

Toward the development of therapeutic expertise, or technical skills, a clinician needs to learn to effectively develop and utilize the therapeutic system, which includes recognizing and mastering his personal themes within clinical transactions. Therapeutic material reveals underlying themes in the therapist's life which both parallel and/or diverge from the client's issues. Certain themes which elicit practitioner issues of both a positive and negative nature need to be monitored. These themes, connected with the specific characteristics of the therapeutic system, create the treatment milieu. Within this context, there is a facet of the interface between the therapist's own life and that of his clients/families that seems to be at the heart of understanding the utilization of the therapeutic relationship. It has to do with sameness and difference between therapist and client and how they fit together because of their similarities and dissimilarities. *Concinnity*, which indicates the skillful and harmonious adaptation or fitting together of parts, connotes the harmony of a similar therapeutic encounter. *Inconcinnity*, in contrast, denotes inharmonious or dissimilar therapeutic interactions.

The underlying element of this interconnecting process originates from the different life experiences of the participants, including such factors as: socioeconomic status, race, gender, occupation, parenthood, and ethnicity. Such themes and structures evolve on a continuum of past to present, and the temporal orientation is inextricably connected on both the conscious and unconscious level of each participant.

The variety of thematic identifications is an essential resource of the therapeutic process. Each dimension can be both an asset and liability to effective treatment. An understanding of these technical dynamics can increase the clinical avenues for generating therapeutic change, as well as allay the practitioner's anxiety, which is frequently attendant in transactions with both concinnity and inconcinnity. Therapists can learn to employ concinnity and inconcinnity in the development of the therapeutic system for the benefit of the client and positive treatment outcome. These harmonious and inharmonious aspects of the practitioner's and client's lives are "givens" in every therapeutic system. A clinician who understands these dynamics can learn to exercise them effectively. Each aspect is both potentially an asset and a liability.

Concinnity

Advantages. The concinnuous therapist and client have similar frames of reference, social symbolism and a common basis for understanding, responding to and caring about issues, for example, when both the client and therapist have lost a parent(s) at an early age. In each person's life, as in therapy, a number of issues and dynamics evolve from this fundamental loss. Concinnity increases the therapist's ability to empathize and join with his client. It can create an immediate attraction and bond. Concinnity is particularly useful when the therapist has experienced a problem similar to the patient's, and successfully resolved it in his own life. The therapist can use the map of his own failures to understand the client.

Disadvantages. On the other hand, sameness can lead to an overidentification that induces blindness and reinforces mutually shared, perhaps dysfunctional, patterns which can induce stagnation and even acting out, well beyond the awareness or intention of the participants. This aspect of personal projection can cause the client to become stuck at the same place the therapist is unable to change. Additionally, the therapist may not expect growth or hold the client truly accountable for movement. If the therapist has, in fact, solved a similar issue to the client's, it can dispose him to be intolerant to others for what he has already conquered in himself, as with the well-known cured "smoker's syndrome." The practitioner's symmetry with a client can cause him not to observe clearly the unique aspects of the client which distinguish the self from the other. The resulting lack of curiosity is deadly to a successful treatment outcome.

Inconcinnity

Advantages. Differences between therapist and client can create a certain objectivity and distance which can be most useful. For example, a therapist who has not experienced a problematic dependency may feel unfettered by a dependent mother/child relationship struggle, and be able to delve into the family with greater freedom. He does not have a need to defend himself and is not looking for the expected. In dissimilar therapist/client dynamics, it is less likely that they will have overlapping dysfunctional pathology and coping patterns. The therapist may be more able to find ways to connect with a client's differences in a complementary fashion that will supply the client with what he needs to take a step toward change. This dynamic can also provide the excitement of differences and the possibility of new learning and extending one's knowledge and horizons.

Disadvantages. A major problem with the inconcinnuous relationship dynamic can be a lack of understanding and basis for connecting between the therapist and client. The issue may be so foreign to a therapist that he has no personal instinct to guide himself and the process in the pursuit of change. Therapists who do not challenge themselves to delve into unknown territories are particularly vulnerable.

Ideally, a therapist needs to have the personal sense of self and its consequent freedom (internal skills) to be both sympathetic and insistent, objective and personally resonant with a family. To do so, he needs to develop the technical expertise to use his sameness and difference with clients to more fully understand, relate to, and effectively intervene in the client system. A clinician needs to have sufficient mastery over himself and his own life experiences to enable the development of a useful therapeutic system. Thus, the practitioner enhances his ability to apply treatment strategies because of his own personal differentiation and the latitude that results from a productive therapeutic relationship. These external or technical skills are required, along with a conceptual framework and useful theoretical maps regarding therapeutic change and intervention. In other words, in psychotherapy a therapist will have something of both the patient and doctor in him. Here lies the purpose of training for the person of the therapist. *The personal training of the therapist, in contrast to personal therapy, is aimed at schooling self and changing self to be able to work more effectively within a relationship with clients/families rather than to primarily enhance one's personal life.*

IMPLICATIONS FOR TRAINING

The development and enhancement of the person of the therapist is a lifelong effort for the clinician. Like learning, essentially there is no end to the process. Similarly, the resolution and development of the therapist's own family life is an infinite, challenging and ongoing process. Certainly, developmental stages in the therapist's own life will elicit different responses, learning and reintegrating of both personal and family dynamics. Efforts in this dimension develop a therapist's *internal* or personal skills. In addition, the therapist needs training that is directly related to his professional goal of using himself effectively in the implementation of therapy and the acquisition of *external* or technical skills.

A central objective for clinical training, then, is to assist the practitioner in his development of the *therapeutic self*, or the part of the person of the therapist which he utilizes within the therapeutic context. This therapeutic self must be congruent with the clinician's *personal self*, which has its identity rooted in his family life. Cultivation of a practitioner's therapeutic self, which is changed, molded or added to within the therapeutic context, enhances one's technical expertise and clinical discipline. Thus, a therapist has an increased ability to depend upon and trust himself as he faces the many unknowns that clients present.

In the training of a therapist, the task is to help a clinician to master himself and his technical skills within the context of conducting therapy. The management of personal self, for the purpose of doing therapy, implies the ability to translate the self into therapeutic action. The therapist has to be trained in how to use himself within a specific theoretical framework and set of techniques, and to develop his own personal therapeutic style.

The process of developing external skills attends to the here and now context of a therapist's interactions with his clients. This, coupled with the practitioner's use of self, is the vital bridge in clinical training. For example, Jay needed help to see himself in his alcoholic client and to reach out to him. He needed assistance to know how to disclose the part of himself that would help diminish his client's defensiveness with him. With the family Jay was treating, he could see his relationship with his own father in the family's father-son struggle. He attempted to draw them together as he wished he could have experienced his own father. Jay was able to usefully inject his personal longing for closeness into the emotional environment of this family which assisted their effort to communicate affection to one another.

Part of the discipline Jay needed was to stay on a track on which he was unaccustomed to travelling.

For Jay it was evident that fundamental change in his relationship with his individual client and in his treatment of the family would have been difficult without the exploration he made of his own family life. As a result of the training interventions, Jay revised his outlook of his father's personal worth and disposition toward him. He gained a more sympathetic understanding of his mother's and sister's behavior, and his took steps to reconnect with them. Jay also intensified his efforts to risk himself emotionally in his relationship with his wife. After giving attention to, and learning more about his own family, Jay was on his way to altering some of his personal themes and consequent structures in his family relationships.

Training the therapist requires identifying issues that concern him about his own family life, and helping him to understand how they are affecting his therapeutic competence. A clinician needs help in changing his approach to his personal life and utilizing his personal victories, struggles and defeats to maximize his therapeutic impact. The past and present in his family of origin and family of procreation, as indicated, are his primary textbooks.

Toward the goal of personal development of the practitioner, therapy for the clinician can be a useful tool. In addition, training conducted in a group context, as illustrated by Jay's transcript, can multiply the learning and subsequent reverberations for not only one trainee, but for a number of people. In addition, the bonds and relationships among the group members enhance and extend the learning process. Additionally, the group creates a parallel arena for the development of the trainee's relationship and collaborative skills (Aponte & Winter, 1987).

In brief, training for therapists' internal and external skills involves:

1. Discovering and understanding one's own personal themes and structures.
2. Resolving issues related to those themes where possible, that is, accepting what one cannot change about one's current life and self, which leads to a transformation of perceptions, relationships and individual psychological functioning.
3. Developing a professional *meta-structure* in relation to one's personal life, that is, creating a perspective about one's life and evolving an approach to using self that is tailored to the clinician's therapeutic self and professional functioning.

The creation of a meta-structure involves the therapist visualizing the treatment context as a safe sanctuary for his psychological self. Here he can *vicariously* observe parts of his own history, family relationships, individual psychology and personal problems in the lives of the people he is treating. He does not have to risk his own personal relationships to resolve these issues within the conduct of his work. The therapist's task is to help and support others to take risks and to effectively address issues in the client's life (Aponte & Winter, 1987). Furthermore, in the *direct* relationship in which a therapist interacts with clients, his personal risk is limited by the boundaries of his professional task. He need only go so far in what he does and becomes with his clients as the solution of the problem requires, and his professional ethics permit.

This safety gives the therapist the freedom to learn how to work with the concinnity and inconcinnity in his relationships with clients' lives. He learns how to use common background as a bridge in a relationship. He becomes adept at employing the distance created by their differences to benignly inquire into and explore areas of the client's behavior patterns or value system, thus making it more acceptable to expect from a client unaccustomed behavior. Essentially, one learns how to be a foreign guide to a client in a strange land.

CONCLUSION

In sum, training needs to assist the practitioner in his identification of his unique personal attributes and style as well as to facilitate his resolution of familial issues. Additionally, it must build a bridge between the therapist's internal skills or personal integration of self and his external skills or technical interventions within the therapeutic system. Essentially, the *Person/Practice* model, as the transcripts with Jay depict, helps fill in the gaps and create links between the different contexts of the therapist's life, his clinical work, family of origin, and family of procreation. The understanding and mastery of the connection between a therapist's clinical work with his family or origin and family of procreation provides the wellspring for the therapeutic process.

BIBLIOGRAPHY

Aponte, H. J., & Winter, J. E. (1987). The person and practice of the therapist: Treatment and training. *Journal of Psychotherapy and the Family*, *3*(1). In M. Baldwin & V. Satir (Eds.), *The use of self in therapy*. New York: Haworth.

Bandler, R., & Grinder, J. (1975). *The structure of magic*. Palo Alto, CA: Science and Behavior.

Boszormenyi-Nagy, I., & Spark, G. (1973). *Invisible loyalties*. New York: Harper and Row.

Bowen, M. (1971-1974). Murray Bowen family therapy seminars. Seminar presentations at the Medical College of Virginia, Richmond, VA.

Bowen, M. (1972). Toward a differentiation of self in one's own family. In James L. Framo (Ed.), *Family interaction* (pp. 111-173). New York: Springer.

Bowen, M. (1978). *Family therapy in clinical practice.* New York: Jason Aronson.

Erickson, M. (1977, October). Clinical hypnosis: Training and supervision seminar. Eight day seminar, Phoenix, AZ.

Freud, S. (1957). The future prospects of psycho-analytic therapy. In J. Strachey (Ed. and Trans.), *The standard edition of the complete psychological works of Sigmund Freud* (Vol. XI, pp. 144-145). London: Hogarth Press. (Original work published in 1910).

Freud, S. (1964). Analysis terminable and interminable. In J. Strachey (Ed. and Trans.) *The standard edition of the complete psychological works of Sigmund Freud* (Vol. XXIII, p. 249). London: Hogarth Press. (Original work published in 1937).

Gurman, A. S., & Kniskern, D. P. (1981). Family therapy outcome research: Knowns and unknowns. In A. S. Gurman & D. P. Kniskern (Eds.), *Handbook of family therapy* (pp. 742-775). New York: Brunner/Mazel.

Haley, J. (1973). *Uncommon therapy.* New York: W. W. Norton.

Haley, J. (1980). *Leaving home.* New York: McGraw-Hill.

Kaslow, F. W. (Ed.). (1984a). *Psychotherapy with psychotherapists.* New York: Haworth.

Kaslow, F. W. (1984b). Treatment of marital and family therapists. In F. W. Kaslow (Ed.), *Psychotherapy with psychotherapists* (pp. 79-102). New York: Haworth.

Minuchin, S. (1980, Vol. IV, No. 3). [Interview by Richard Simon (Ed.)] A therapy of challenge. *Family Therapy Practice Network Newsletter* (pp. 5-11).

Nerin, W. F. (1986). *Family reconstruction: Long day's journey into light.* New York: W. W. Norton.

Pillari, V. (1986). *Pathways to family myths.* New York: Brunner/Mazel.

Satir, V. S. (1972). *Conjoint family therapy* (rev. ed.). Palo Alto, CA: Science and Behavior.

Satir, V. (1982, October). Focus for change: The therapist and the system. Three day seminar under the auspices of the Family Institute of Virginia, McLean, VA.

Satir, V., & Baldwin, M. (1983). *Satir step by step.* Palo Alto, CA: Science and Behavior.

Satir, V. (1986, January). [Interview with Joan E. Winter, Executive Director, *Family research project*]. Unpublished transcript.

Satir, V. (1987). The therapist's story. *Journal of Psychotherapy and the Family, 3*(1). In M. Baldwin & V. Satir (Eds.), *The use of self in therapy.* New York: Haworth.

Watzlawick, P. (1984, June). The problems of change: The change of problems. Symposium conducted at the Eastern Virginia Medical School, Norfolk, VA.

Whitaker, Carl A. (1982). Hypnosis and family depth therapy. In J. K. Zeig (Ed.), *Ericksonian approaches to hypnosis and psychotherapy, 1980* (pp. 491-504). New York: Brunner/Mazel.

Williamson, D. S. (1978). New life at the graveyard: A method of therapy for individuation from a dead former parent. *Journal of Marital and Family Counseling, 4,* 93-101.

Winter, J. E. (1986). [Family Research Project: Family Therapy Outcome Study of Bowen, Haley, Satir]. Unpublished 1979-1980 interview transcripts.

The Impact of the Therapist's Personal Family Life on the Ability to Establish Viable Therapeutic Alliances in Family and Marital Therapy

Donald R. Catherall
William M. Pinsof

SUMMARY. The therapeutic alliance formed by a family therapist is a complex phenomenon in which the therapist must ally with the system as well as with the individual members of the system. Further, many individual members may be in conflict with one another and highly sensitive to the therapist's alliance with the other members of the system. Traditional definitions of the alliance in individual therapy are not adequate to describe these multiple levels on which the alliance is manifested. The therapeutic alliance established by family therapists is conceptualized as occurring between two interpersonal systems, the patient system and the therapist system. The therapist system includes indirect elements from the therapist's professional and personal life.

The therapist's personal life includes both immediate and remote elements in the form of the therapist's current family life as well as family of origin experiences. These elements impact on the therapist's alliances in a variety of ways, such as coloring the therapist's ideas about fairness, normalcy and the appropriateness of roles in family life. This paper examines the possible influence of several dimensions of the therapist's personal family life: family roles, the family emotional atmosphere, the extent of triangulation, the degree of differentiation, unresolved interpersonal conflicts, and styles of coping with family developmental stages.

Donald R. Catherall, PhD, is a clinical psychologist and family therapist. He is Clinical Training Coordinator at the Center for Family Studies/Family Institute of Chicago, a division of Northwestern Memorial Hospital. Dr. Catherall is Associate in Clinical Psychiatry at Northwestern University Medical School. William M. Pinsof, PhD, is a clinical psychologist and family therapist. He is Director of the Center for Family Studies/Family Institute of Chicago, a division of Northwestern Memorial Hospital. Dr. Pinsof is Associate Professor in Clinical Psychiatry at Northwestern University Medical School.

The therapeutic alliance is a concept that is clinically useful in all forms of psychotherapy. The concept refers to the quality of the collaborative relationship between therapist and patient. The idea of an alliance evolved in individual therapy and thus its definition is usually conceived in individually oriented terms. The concept becomes more complicated when applied to conjoint therapies because the therapist must deal with different people simultaneously. Therapists must consider the impact of their relationship with any one individual upon their relationship with the others. Additionally, therapists must consider their relationship with the system as a whole as well as with each individual member. Thus, the therapeutic alliance is a more complicated phenomenon when considered in the context of the multiple levels of relationship inherent in family and marital therapies.

The alliance concept has been discussed extensively, particularly in the analytic literature. Psychoanalytic clinicians often evaluate their cases by considering whether they have a good therapeutic alliance with their patients (Chessick, 1974; Kanzer, 1975; Langs, 1975). Some family therapists have utilized the concept of the therapeutic alliance (Kramer, 1977) but only recently has there been a concerted effort to elaborate an explicit theory about the role of the therapeutic alliance in marital and family therapy (Gurman, 1982; Dryden & Hunt, 1985a, 1986b; Rutan & Smith, 1985; Pinsof & Catherall, 1986). A number of family therapists have emphasized the importance of the therapist maintaining a good working relationship with the various members of the patient system (Boszormenyi-Nagy, 1965; Ackerman, 1966; Satir, 1967; Minuchin, 1974; Sluzki, 1975; Davatz, 1981).

A major trend in the individual psychotherapy literature has been to focus on the therapist as a person. By and large, this trend has not explicitly influenced nor been related to the alliance literature. Theory on the therapist as a person has focused on three major areas. The first is the area of countertransference. An extensive literature has accrued within psychoanalysis dealing with the analyst's personal responses to the patient and the ways in which those responses can influence the analysis or therapy for better or for worse. The second major area concerns the personality style of the therapist. This area has been the subject of numerous studies examining the effects of therapist personality variables on the outcome of treatment. The third area pertains to the concept of self-disclosure, referring to interventions in which the therapist reveals personal information to the patient. The literature on therapist self-disclosure has been neither extensive nor conclusive (Parloff, Waskow, & Wolfe, 1978; Orlinsky & Howard, 1978).

With the exception of some research on therapist demographic variables (Parloff et al., 1978), the concept of the therapist's personal family life, both past and present, has been largely ignored within the psychotherapy literature. The area has received some attention within the field of family therapy (Charney, 1982; Kaslow, 1984) but there is virtually no body of research (Gurman & Kniskern, 1978).

This paper will consider the impact of the therapist's personal family life on the therapeutic alliance in family and marital therapy. We will begin with an examination of the concept of the therapeutic alliance and its application in conjoint, systemically oriented therapies.

CONCEPT OF THERAPEUTIC ALLIANCE

The Analytic Perspective

The concept of the alliance originated in a classic paper by Sterba called "The Fate of the Ego in Analytic Therapy" (1934). This paper proposed that a patient's ego develops a dissociative split in psychoanalysis and the analyst effects an alliance with one part of the split ego "against the powerful forces of instinct and repression" (1934, p. 119). Bibring (1937) further developed the idea that it was the healthy part of the ego that allied with the analyst and he coined the phrase "therapeutic alliance." This trend led to the work of Hartmann, who conceived of the healthy part of the ego as constituting a conflict-free sphere (1939).

It remained a controversy as to whether the alliance is established only with the healthy, conflict-free sphere of the ego or whether the patient's transference motives and feelings were involved. Freud (1912) had suggested that only transference could provide sufficient motivation for the patient to maintain the attachment to the analyst in the face of powerful resistances. However, the transference origin of the bond is countered by modern authors who have shown that the patient's real relationship with the analyst or therapist provides real and current reasons for the patient to attach to the person of the therapist (Greenson, 1965; Greenson & Wexler, 1969). Although some authors have taken extreme positions on this subject, most have come to agree that both aspects of the patient's personality are involved (Dickes, 1975; Curtis, 1979).

The acknowledgement of the role of the real relationship helped turn the focus back to the therapist. Some authors argued that analysts must go beyond their usual analytic role in order to facilitate the development of an alliance with neurotic patients (Zetzel, 1956; Kohut,

1984). Even analytic authors who disagreed with this violation of classical technique conceded that such procedures were frequently necessary in the treatment of more severely disturbed patients (Curtis, 1979).

The psychoanalytic psychotherapies emphasize the development of transference for two reasons: (1) in order to engage the patient's collaboration and provide the leverage for change, and (2) to bring the patient's interpersonal difficulties into the therapy where they can be examined directly. In family and couple therapies, the transference attachment and interpersonal difficulties are brought into the therapy primarily in the form of the relationships between the members of the patient system. Thus, the degree to which a transference attachment to the therapist is necessary may differ according to the patient context, that is, pre-existing transference relationships. The therapeutic alliance with a family therapist *may* rest largely upon the non-transference elements of the relationship.

The Systemic Perspective

The systemic perspective widens the viewing field to consider the entire interpersonal context in which the alliance appears, including both the patient system and the therapist system (Pinsof & Catherall, 1986). The family therapist must maintain an alliance with individuals who may be in conflict with each other while simultaneously maintaining an alliance with them as parts of a greater system, i.e., a couple or family. The therapist does not initially meet the individuals as individuals, they are met as a family or a couple. They define themselves in relation to each other, not the way they might if encountered alone.

The entrance of the therapist can upset the system's homeostatic equilibrium and stimulate negative feedback mechanisms. The clinician must be careful not to grossly violate the families' meta-rules, the rules concerning proper thought, feeling, and action (Watzlawick, Beavin, & Jackson, 1967). These family rules may not be explicitly expressed or upheld by only one member; they are a product of the system as a whole. The therapist must perceive and react to the rules of the system in order to maintain an alliance with the system as a whole.

The patient system. We have attempted to extend the concept of the therapeutic alliance into the family field, both theoretically and empirically (Pinsof & Catherall, 1986). In doing so, we were immediately confronted with the issue of determining who is involved in the alliance. Family therapists tend to see different members of the family at different times, some members being more peripherally involved in the sessions than others. We therefore found it necessary to speak of the alliance as occurring between the patient system and the therapist system, which together "consist of all the people that can influence the change process" (Pinsof & Catherall, 1986, p. 139).

The family therapist forms an alliance with the entire patient system, rather than solely with individuals. The patient system "consists of all the human systems . . . that are or may be involved in the maintenance or resolution of the presenting problem" (Pinsof, 1983, p. 20). The patient system is a social system and operates according to systemic rules which influence the individuals' functioning (Haley, 1967; Jackson, 1957). In effect, the therapist must form alliances with family members both individually and as a system.

Taking a systemic perspective in conceptualizing the alliance entails thinking differently about individual therapy as well. The therapeutic alliance is seen as occurring between two individuals who exist within a larger system of relationships that affects each of the individuals. Attitudes, loyalties, rewards, guilts and other pressures are brought to bear on the individual patient by his/her significant others. The development and maintenance of a therapeutic alliance is certainly different if the significant others support the therapy than if they denigrate it. That aspect of the alliance that pertains to the therapist's relationship with the patient system of significant others is bidirectional, the alliance is also affected by the therapist's attitudes concerning the patient's significant others.

The therapist system. The therapist system consists of the interpersonal system that influences the therapist in his/her conduct of the therapy. This can include professional peers and coworkers, as well as agency policies and norms. On a direct level, the behavior of receptionists or other staff members at the therapist's office can have a clear influence on the patient's experience of the therapy. When clinic therapists attribute their behavior to clinic policy, they are actively including the agency in their relationships with their patients. The power of some patients' transference to institutions has long been recognized as a factor in their ability to commit to their therapy.

The therapist system also possesses more indirect elements. These include the therapist's significant relationships, which contribute to therapist attitudes about normalcy, fairness, and the appropriateness of roles. The indirect aspects of the therapist system are usually invisible in forms of therapy that discourage self-disclosure, high therapist activity, and directiveness. The more disclosing, active and directive therapists are, the more their attitudes and values become visible. Family therapists tend to be more self-revealing, active and directive than individual therapists (Pinsof, 1986) and the influence of their personal family life is consequently more visible in the therapy.

The issues encountered in the therapist's personal life influence therapist sensitivity and perspective vis-à-vis the problems presented by patients. A therapist involved in a conflictual relationship is likely to take a different view of marital problems than a therapist who is unattached. This final aspect of the therapist system is of particular significance in family and marital therapy, where therapists are confronted with both sides of disputes and cannot simply empathize with an individual's unique perspective. Some family and marital therapists often feel forced to take a position concerning conflicts and thus their own personal experiences tend to enter the treatment. The second half of this paper will take an in-depth look at those aspects of the therapist's personal life which are most likely to impact on the therapist's perspective.

Research on the Therapeutic Alliance

The history of alliance research can be traced back to earlier research on therapist-offered conditions (Rogers, 1957; Truax, 1966). This direction in research tended to emphasize the therapist's personal qualities. Strupp included the person of the therapist in his appraisal of thenonspecific factors that influence treatment (1970). He later stressed that technique plays an equally important role (1973, 1973a, 1978). He concluded that technique is only effective insofar as it forms an integral part of the therapist as a person. Strupp's work suggests that alliance measures must concentrate on the patient's perception of both the therapist's personal qualities and technical skills.

This issue was also developed in Frank's (1961) discussion of the therapist's power to heal. Frank posits that the patient's belief in the healer's personal power is an essential element in any healing relationship. This element is sometimes discussed in terms of the therapist's credibility. For example, parents sometimes distrust therapists without children because the parents do not believe the therapist has sufficient experiential understanding of the problems of childrearing.

Another important aspect in the research leading towards alliance measures was the increased interest in the patient's experience. This focus was highlighted by Carl Rogers (1957) and the client-centered investigators. In his discussion of his Relationship Inventory, Barrett-

Lennard states that it is the client's experience of his therapist's response which is the "primary locus of therapeutic influence" (1962, p. 2).

Many studies since the early 1950s have focused on variables in the patient-therapist relationship but it was not until the 1970s that the alliance concept was operationalized. A number of alliance measures have emerged since 1975. The first and longest running study dealing with the alliance is the Penn Psychotherapy Project (Luborsky, 1976). All of the alliance studies to date have shown some degree of effectiveness at measuring a positive working relationship and predicting better treatment outcomes within individual therapy (Marziali, Marmar, & Krupnik, 1981; Morgan, Luborsky, Crits-Christoph, Curtis, & Solomon, 1982).

Operationalizing the therapeutic alliance. The alliance has been operationalized differently by the many investigators. Some have focused on the patient's experience of therapist helpfulness while others have sought to isolate the spirit of collaboration. Luborsky (1976) sought to establish subdimensions of the alliance. He conceived of two types of helping alliances: Type I, which entails the patient's experience of the therapist as warm, helpful and supportive, and Type II, which entails the patient's experience of collaboration with the therapist. Luborsky's more recent efforts have collapsed this distinction and focus primarily on the patient's experience of being helped (Morgan et al., 1982).

Another recent patient self-report instrument in the Working Alliance Inventory (W.A.I.), a questionnaire developed by Horvath and Greenberg (1982). The W.A.I. is based on Bordin's (1975) paper, "The Generalizability of the Psychoanalytic Concept of the Working Alliance." Bordin proposed that the alliance could best be operationalized by subdividing it into three components: tasks, bonds, and goals. Specifically, he was referring to the existence of a personal bond between therapist and patient, agreement of the goals of therapy, and the patient's perception that the tasks of therapy are relevant to his/her concerns and fit his/her expectations about therapy. Horvath and Greenberg found the task dimension to account for the greatest part of the predictable outcome variance.

A systemic alliance perspective. None of the existing alliance measures accounted for the presence of others in the therapy. The Integrative Psychotherapy Alliance Scales (I.P.A.S.) were developed to address this deficit and incorporate a systems perspective (Pinsof & Catherall, 1986). The scales are composed of three instruments, each being a form adapted to one of the three patient contexts of individual, couple, and family therapy. Separate scales were developed in order to accommodate the different interpersonal composition of the three therapeutic contexts.

The three scales are all based on the same concept of the alliance and derive from two theoretical dimensions – Content and Interpersonal System. The Content dimension refers to the thematic categories of the alliance. The three categories of the Content dimension are Tasks, Goals, and Bonds, and are patterned after Horvath and Greenberg's use of Bordin's operational definition of the working alliance in individual psychotherapy. The Interpersonal System dimension refers to the levels of the interpersonal systems involved in the alliance. The three categories of the Interpersonal System dimension are Self-Therapist, Other-Therapist and Group-Therapist, referring to the therapist's relationship with (1) the individual patient, (2) the significant others, and (3) the system or family as a whole. Initial results with the three scales have shown good reliability (r = .84) and an ability to predict outcome (Catherall, 1984).

Our choice of alliance dimensions reflects our belief that the alliance is manifested among the three subdimensions (Tasks, Goals, Bonds) across the three systemic levels (the Whole System, the Interpersonal, the Intrapersonal). The degree to which the dimensions differ in their influence will vary according to the systemic level and the nature of the problem. It is possible for factors to favor the alliance at one level while being deleterious for the alliance at another level. For example, the need for an individual to differentiate may compete with the need for the family to maintain cohesion. The goals of the therapist's alliance with the individual may run counter to the goals of the therapist's alliance with the whole system. The therapist's task of helping the individual differentiate may damage the goal component of the therapist's alliance with the whole system. Ultimately, *we believe it is the alliance with the whole system that is most crucial.*

Clearly, it is not easy for a family therapist to establish and maintain a positive therapeutic alliance across all three levels of the patient system. The therapist must contend with different and sometimes conflicting configurations in the structure of the alliance. The situation is made even more difficult when one considers the complexities of the therapist system, including the impact of the therapist's professional life as well as personal family life (Skynner, 1981).

IMPACT OF THERAPIST'S PERSONAL FAMILY LIFE

The therapist's personal family life appears to exert an important influence on the therapeutic alliance, particularly in marital and family therapy. The remainder of this paper will attempt to elucidate the nature of this aspect of the therapist system. There are numerous parameters of all families that shape family life in often invisible ways. We learn our ideas about normality and fairness from our experiences in our own families and this knowledge colors our perceptions.

It is beyond the scope of this article to present a comprehensive coverage of the parameters of family life that impact on the therapist system and thereby influence the alliance. Instead, we have chosen to concentrate on those aspects of family life which have gained considerable attention from family therapists in their clinical evaluation of families. These parameters include: family roles, the family emotional atmosphere, the extent of triangulation, the degree of differentiation, unresolved interpersonal conflicts, and styles of coping with family developmental stages.

We are first confronted with these experiences in our families of origin, where we learn our basic attitudes. Later, these attitudes are amended and elaborated in our current families. We will examine the various parameters of family life beginning with family of origin experiences and moving to current family life. We will conclude with a discussion of the interface between client issues, the therapist's own family issues and the effect on the therapist's ability to form viable therapeutic alliances with the family.

Family of Origin

Every family has a unique personality that leaves its mark on each child that develops in that environment. When there is more than one child, each adopts particular characteristics that allow him or her a distinctly unique identity within the family (Minuchin, 1974). As the child begins to relate to a larger social world, the "within family" identity is altered to accommodate to the way the child sees him/herself in relation to the outside world. But many aspects of the family life continue to influence the child's perceptions of self and others. This is true in two senses, the child (1) continues to carry basic perceptions learned in the family environment, and (2) continues to be a member of the family of origin and is influenced in an ongoing way, even if the child is an adult and no longer living at home.

Family Roles

Everyone plays a role in their family. Some roles can be positive and contribute to a child's character development; some can be negative and interfere with a child's development. Positive roles are usually based on the individual's predisposition and facilitate problem solving in the family (Metcoff & Whitaker, 1982). The extent to which a role is viewed as pathological depends upon the degree to which the individual sacrifices their true nature. Excessive parental projections prevent children from having much influence upon their choice of role and result in irrational role assignments (Framo, 1982). Family pathology often dictates that children are thrust into roles that are inappropriate to their developmental level, such as when children are expected to act like parents or spouses.

The common denominator of pathological family roles is that members develop them in order to take care of the family (Watzlawick, Beavin, & Jackson, 1967), either for the sake of other individuals (such as someone with very low self-esteem), relationships (such as unresolved marital conflicts), or the whole family (such as a family that carries unresolved grief). Yet many of the positive roles which individuals learn in their families of origin are also acquired in order to take care of the family. In either case, individuals will be influenced by their early family roles in their future relations, particularly when they encounter family constellations that resemble their family of origin.

The influence of family roles upon the therapist. Roles are reciprocal and the therapist is induced to fill vacant reciprocal roles in families as a result of the family's need and the therapist's own comfort with those roles. The family therapist is often pressured to assume many of the inappropriate roles assigned to children, such as caretaker, substitute spouse, or substitute parent. Miller (1981) has suggested that people who choose to be psychotherapists do so because they already have assumed a caretaker role in their family of origin. Whether they did have such roles or not, therapists are inevitably going to be influenced by their own family roles when they are dealing with family pathology. They may find themselves falling back into family roles that they have managed to transcend since leaving home. And they may find themselves having emotional reactions to client families when they sense the pressure to assume inappropriate roles (Kramer, 1985).

The kind of therapeutic alliance forged by the family therapist will be influenced by the kind of roles they learned in their families of origin. Therapists who played important roles in protecting their families are likely to re-assume these roles unless they make conscious efforts to avoid doing so. The assumption of these roles may well affect the goals the therapists can pursue, the tasks the therapist can engage in, and the bonds the therapist can develop and sustain with each family member and with the family as a whole.

The role which the therapist is induced to re-assume can be either helpful or harmful to the therapeutic alliance. The therapist may assume an over-competent rescuer style that interferes with the therapeutic goal of helping the family develop their own problem solving capacities. Or a therapist rescuer may be able to support a scapegoated member and facilitate the therapeutic task of openly discussing conflicts. Similarly, a former caretaker may avoid the therapeutic task by accepting false issues and avoiding confrontations with certain members. But a therapist caretaker may be quite helpful with overly conflictual families where the therapeutic task has more to do with the development of acceptance and support. As therapist, a former parentified child may ignore breaches in generational boundaries and not challenge inappropriate role expectations of children, thus avoiding the therapeutic task and developing a poor bond with the children. Or a former parentified child may be able to provide the kind of support and guidance of a parent that is sometimes part of the therapeutic task and bond required with some systems, such as with a single parent who lacks sufficient resources to cope with childrearing demands.

Therapists who were assigned inappropriate roles in their own families may overreact to these issues in patient families by becoming overly combative and unempathic. A former parentified child may accept excessive irresponsibility by the children and fail to support the parents. In order for therapists to avoid these pitfalls, they must begin by retrospective examination of the roles they played in their own family. There is no absolute freedom from roles but an informed therapist can have greater choice over which roles to assume, when to assume them, and with whom.

The Emotional Atmosphere

Every family possesses its own distinct emotional atmosphere; some are openly loving while others are distant and reserved; some are very close with siblings maintaining involvement into adult life while others are not close and members drift apart. Two variables can be used to describe the emotional atmosphere of a family, emotional expressiveness (Vaughn & Leff, 1976) and cohesion (Sprenkle & Olson,

1978). Each variable describes a continuum of experiencing from low to high.

Highly expressive families openly display their emotions, particularly in regard to one another. Some families are expressive about certain emotions but not others, such as pseudomutual families that avoid conflict (Wynne, Ryckoff, Day, & Hirsch, 1958). Families that are constricted in their ability to express sadness are often blocked in the grieving process and are unable to mourn their losses (Paul, 1969). Families that avoid the expression of intimacy are often inhibited in their ability to provide emotional support during times of need. Families that are more expressive may be somewhat better equipped to deal with grief, conflict, and intimacy; however, research suggests that some families can be overly expressive and create an atmosphere that is detrimental to certain vulnerable members (Vaughn, Snyder, Jones, Freeman, & Falloon, 1984).

Family cohesion may be related to family expressiveness. Families that are able to express their feelings of intimacy and conflict tend to be families that are close and value their relationships with one another. Such families may be better able to sustain individual members through personal crises, such as job loss, divorce or exposure to trauma. Conversely, families that are low on cohesiveness may not be experienced by individual members as a potential resource during times of difficulty. As with emotional expressiveness, excessive cohesion can lead to dysfunctional behavior and moderate levels are considered most conducive to affect functioning (Sprenkel & Olson, 1978).

Marital and family therapists are frequently in the position of trying to help their clients deal with issues of grief, conflict or intimacy. Therapists are immediately confronted with their own expectations about how these issues are to be approached. Despite their training, the intense emotions bound up in these issues may prompt therapists to respond according to the styles they learned in their own family of origin. Clinicians who come from families that are low on expressiveness and cohesiveness may have difficulty with intense emotion and may fail to recognize the impact of familial relationships. Therapists who come from families that are high on both variables may be unempathic to a family's difficulty in processing emotional issues and they may misinterpret such difficulties as resistance to treatment.

When the presenting problem involves the intense emotions associated with grief, conflict or intimacy, the task dimension of the alliance often requires the therapist to create a facilitative emotional atmosphere in the sessions. Doing so may conflict with family rules and threaten the therapist's alliance with the whole system. Affect-avoidant therapists may not be able to tolerate the intense emotional atmosphere.

Intrapersonal levels of the alliance may also be threatened when family members possess catastrophic fears concerning the expression of certain intense emotions. For example, individuals who have been traumatized are usually fearful of a loss of control brought on by the experiencing of suppressed emotions (Catherall, 1986). In such cases, the individual may only be willing to explore the suppressed emotions because of the strength of the alliance bond with the therapist and the individual's belief in the therapist's personal power, an aspect of both the task and bond components of the alliance.

Unearthing conflicts can disrupt the interpersonal patterns in a family and threaten a family's cohesion. A therapist may see this as a necessary step in resolving the presenting problem but find that the family fails to see the task as relevant. For example, a marital couple may deny any relationship between their unresolved conflicts and a symptomatic child. Establishing the relationship between their conflicts and the child's symptom is necessary before the task of resolving the conflict is accepted by the parents. This takes time and the therapist must rely on other aspects of the alliance while building a case to justify working on the marital relationship. If the therapist comes from a very expressive family and pursues conflicts prematurely, the client family may feel unsafe and terminate. In effect, the therapist will have failed to deal with the tasks of the alliance by not providing a safe emotional atmosphere.

It behooves therapists to increase their knowledge about the emotional atmosphere of their families of origin and to pursue increased flexibility in their approach to such issues with client families. Though we have emphasized the positive benefits of moderately high degrees of expressiveness and cohesion, it should be noted that these do not always foster a positive alliance. A similarity between the emotional atmosphere of the therapist's family of origin and a client family may facilitate the formation of the alliance, regardless of whether the atmosphere is high or low in expressiveness and cohesion. It is easy to superimpose the expressive atmosphere of one's family of origin onto client families without sufficient regard for the anxiety created when expressiveness increases. Contrariwise, therapists from non-expressive, non-cohesive families may be limited in their ability to engage in creating a facilitative emotional atmosphere. This is an area where personal therapy for the therapist may be necessary to overcome narrow expectations about family life.

The Extent of Triangulation

Triangulation refers to the process of bringing a third person into a dyadic issue. The third person is usually pressured to take a position that favors one or the other of the two individuals involved in the dispute and alternately aligns with each (Aponte & VanDeusen, 1981). This often occurs in pathological family systems, the most frequent case being a child who is brought into a marital dispute. Therapists who grew up in families that used traingulation are accustomed to assuming an intermediary role and buffering direct dyadic conflict. They may fear the catastrophic consequences of allowing two individuals to work out their differences directly. They may be insensitive to the inappropriate use of a third party or they may be hypersensitive to any inclusion of a third party. Their experience in their family of origin may lead them to assume a reasonableness to triangulation that prevents them from recognizing its undesirable effects.

The sequelae of triangulation experiences in the therapist's family of origin strike directly at the interpersonal level of the alliance. The issue for the therapist is "Who's side are you on?" The goal is for the therapist to de-triangulate third parties out of conflicts and yet part of the task to accomplish that goal may require that the therapist temporarily be part of a triangle. Therapist may feel a pressure to maintain their alliance bonds with certain individuals by siding with them in disputes. The question of when to participate in a triangle and when to insist that two people work out their own problems is extemely complex; therapist experiences with triangulation in their family of origin can influence this type of clinical decision making.

The Degree of Differentiation

Murray Bowen's concept of differentiation (1961, 1978) refers to the degree of individuation, separateness, independence, autonomy, and individual difference achieved by family members. We are each engaged on a lifelong journey toward achieving greater degrees of differentiation; Bowen contends that we never achieve a totally differentiated state. Poorly differentiated families create individuals who cannot function well outside the family; they are mutually dependent upon one another, though often resentful at the same time.

Individuals from moderately differentiated families can function autonomously but are vulnerable to becoming overly enmeshed and reactive in later relationships. Therapists from such families may unconsciously interfere with their patients' independence by establishing alliances that are based upon a mutual dependence rather than a mutual collaboration. Poorly differentiated therapists may have difficulty establishing a bond that respects individual differences. They might be able to establish a bond with the whole system but not with the individuals. The ability to relate to each person as an individual is an important aspect of the task and bond dimension with enmeshed families.

Adaptability and Coping Style

Every family can be evaluated according to its general level of adaptability (Sprenkle & Olson, 1978) and the coping techniques it commonly employs. Children grow up learning a repertoire of coping mechanisms and acquiring a general level of adaptability which they take into each new situation. Families tend to transmit these approaches over generations. Children must learn to deal with a variety of problems, originating both within themselves and in the environment, including: aggressive impulses, frustration, disabilities, interpersonal conflicts, rejection, loss, limited environmental resources, and traumatic experiences. Maladaptive coping styles, such as resorting to violence or drug use, are learned and passed on in the family of origin. More adaptive styles of coping, such as self-discipline and listening skills, can be learned after leaving home, but nonadaptive methods must be unlearned before they can be effectively replaced. The training of psychotherapists is designed to broaden their repertoire of coping skills and give them a greater range of adaptive options for dealing with problems. However, psychotherapy training often does not spend sufficient time helping therapists unlearn maladaptive coping mechanisms. This is one reason why many training programs emphasize personal psychotherapy for the trainees.

Periods of stress and intensity often push us to respond with our most basic and longstanding coping mechanisms; we may find ourselves not taking advantage of more recently acquired options. Family therapists are frequently confronted with the most stressful and intense problems families face. The therapist's ability to personally understand and relate to a family's problems is a significant factor in building an alliance, but it is also a potential trap that can lead to a nontherapeutic alliance. The therapist can easily become overinvolved and respond with coping mechanisms that are harmful. When family members resort to coping mechanisms that are similar to the therapist's own, past or present, it can cloud the therapist's judgement and objectivity.

This is another area where marital and family therapists are more vulnerable than individual therapists. The individual therapist is exposed to intrapersonal defenses that may echo his or her own style. But the individual patient is usually slow to bring the interpersonal mechanisms into the therapy relationship. The family therapist is exposed quickly to both intrapersonal and interpersonal coping mechanisms in intense situations, which often propel the therapist to respond out of habit rather than out of thoughtfulness.

The coping mechanisms carried from family of origin experiences affect the therapeutic alliance at the task dimension across all three systemic levels. This is an area where therapist's training can carry them only so far, and then the coping style learned consciously and unconsciously in their personal family life tends to be expressed.

Unresolved Transference Issues

The subject of the therapist's own transferences must be addressed in any discussion of contaminants of the alliance. Clearly, it is more difficult for therapists to be empathic to some patients because they stir up negative feelings associated with a similar figure from the therapist's past. When this occurs in a family setting, the therapist is more likely to support pathological configurations, e.g., scapegoating that individual or joining coalitions opposed to him/her. But it can be equally destructive to the alliance if the therapist has unexamined positive transferences to members of the family. The therapist may then ignore such members' participation in maintaining the problems or may encourage the family to act out fantasies and longings from the therapist's past; actions which may be unrealistic for the therapy. For instance, the therapist may strive to establish a close loving relationship between a parent and child in a family that has come to therapy to overcome some other problem. The patient family may not be interested in greater closeness or require it in order to resolve the presenting problem. The therapist's own unresolved issue has thus interfered with the goals dimension of the alliance.

The underlying problem with unresolved countertransference issues is the same in both individual and family treatment. Therapists are like to distort their perceptions and impose their own issues upon patients. However, family therapists are often forced to deal with this situation in a more compelling sense. They do not have the opportunity to slowly observe the situation developing and to prepare for their own reactions. They are confronted with full blown patient transferences and interpersonal issues being enacted within the patient system as soon as the first session begins.

The therapist's unresolved issues can impact all three dimensions of the alliance at all three levels. He or she can have difficulty establishing bonds to transference figures or can have bonds that are based on unresolved transference longings. The therapist may impose idiosyncratic tasks and goals on families because the family's issues resurrect the therapist's issues. The therapist can have countertransferential reactions to individuals, to interpersonal configurations, and to the whole family configuration. Therapists need to be aware of the triggers that stimulate their own issues. Therapist self-understanding can provide considerable insight into the family and can facilitate the development of the therapeutic alliance.

Current Family

The issues stemming from the therapist's family of origin are also relevant in the therapist's current family life. Therapists are influenced by the role they play in their family, by its emotional atmosphere, by the extent of triangulation and differentiation tolerated in their current family, and by the coping styles employed in their family. In particular, therapists are affected by the unresolved issues in their current family relationships. There is an additional dimension in the therapist's current family life which bears on the viability and quality of the alliances they form with client families, the developmental stage of the therapist's current family.

The Family's Experience of the Therapist's Developmental Stage

Family and marital therapists constantly deal with two kinds of intensely emotional relationships among their patients, the issues are manifested between members of an intimate couple, usually husband and wife, and between parents and children. Most people find unexpected changes occur when they enter new levels of their family relationships. Consequently, patients are sensitive to whether the therapist truly appreciates the experience of being married or being a parent. Young therapists who appear to lack life experience are often suspect in the eyes of patients who have already married and borne children. This issue is often broached by questions about the therapist's own life experience, "Are you married?," "Are you divorced?," and "Do you have children?"

These two primary relationships each involve numerous developmental milestones, usually subsumed in the literature under the heading of the family life cycle (McGoldrick & Carter, 1982). Patients may focus on their current developmental issue, challenging the therapist's expertise by implying that the therapist lacks the life experience to understand the subtle nuances. If the therapist fails to demonstrate an appreciation of the patients' experience, then this challenge to the therapist's expertise can weaken the task dimension of the alliance because part of the therapist's task is to be knowledgeable and understand (Pinsof & Catherall, 1986).

The Therapist's Experience of His or Her Own Developmental Stage

The quality of the therapist's immediate close relationships exerts a powerful influence on the therapist's ability to create, sustain, and appropriately elaborate a therapeutic alliance. The existence of problems similar to the patient's can facilitate the task and bond dimensions of the alliance by increasing therapist empathy and understanding. But the existence of similar problems can also bring the therapist's own blind spots into the sessions.

The therapist who encounters a family which seems to mirror the therapist's own current family ("They are just like my spouse and me!") is vulnerable to overidentifying with the "similar" member. The bond developed with such a member can be more distorted by the therapist's narcissistic needs and, paradoxically, lack an empathic appreciation of the individual. Similarly, the therapist is more vulnerable to imposing his or her own goals upon the family and to distorting perceptions of their family members. As a result, the therapist who encounters a mirror family may develop a stronger alliance at the whole system level but a weaker alliance at the intrapersonal and interpersonal levels. Or the therapist may have a stronger alliance at all three levels, depending upon the therapist's ability to control overidentification and use personal experiences for understanding while dealing with personal issues outside of therapy.

This discussion has not been advanced to suggest that every family therapist should be married and have children. But family therapists need to recognize the impact of these life experiences and should familiarize themselves with the vicissitudes of family life. It is important for therapists to recognize the implications of sharing or not sharing life experiences with their patients. Some patients may simply refuse to work with a therapist who does not share these life experiences. Other patients may be less concerned about the lack of common experience, particularly when the therapist is knowledgeable and skillful and shows a desire to understand their specific dynamics and transactional system.

Interface Issues

The therapist's personal family life is actually an aspect of the therapist/patient system and, as such, influences the therapeutic alliance. There are dimensions of the therapist's life of which the family is unaware, such as the degree of differentiation and triangulation, and dimensions which the family might learn about, such as the therapist's own developmental stage. The patient family's knowledge of certain aspects of the therapist's life may strengthen or weaken the alliance. This raises the question of when therapist self-disclosure would be helpful and when it might be destructive to the alliance.

Therapist self-disclosure has not been studied in terms of its effect on the therapeutic alliance but it has been studied in terms of its relationship to outcome. Orlinsky and Howard (1978) note the complexity of this issue, indicating that there are a variety of influential variables, including patient expectations, type of patient, and type of treatment. In a review of studies on the relationship between therapist self-disclosure and client attraction, Strong (1978) reports that interviewers who disclosed similarities to college students were rated as more attractive than interviewers who disclosed dissimilarities. The research from nontherapeutic settings indicates that intimacy develops with self-disclosure in a curvilinear relationship (Cozby, 1973; Gilbert, 1976). A certain amount of disclosure facilitates greater intimacy but excessive disclosure can reduce feelings of intimacy and actually be a "turn-off." This may be particularly true when it is occurring in a session which the patient has paid for.

We believe therapist disclosure of familial similarities may strengthen the alliance but we would caution against excessive disclosure or disclosing unresolved or controversial issues. On the other hand, we believe that disclosure of intense, emotional life events experienced in common with patients will usually strengthen the alliance. This is particularly true of trauma and loss, provided the therapist has grieved and recovered from the event.

The pertinent point in discussing the therapist/patient system is not whether an alliance will be established as much as what kind of alliance. The interface between the alliance and the therapist's personal life can lead to the formation of various therapeutic and nontherapeutic alliances with patient families such as: (1) avoidant or approaching alliances, (2) system maintaining or system changing alliances, and (3) insensitivity to the alliance.

Avoidant or Approaching Alliances

Most families come to therapy because they are not adequately pursuing appropriate pathways for resolving their problem. The therapist can form an alliance with the family which requires everyone, including the therapist, engage in the appropriate tasks or the therapist can form an alliance which allows him/her to participate with the family in avoiding these tasks and instead busying themselves with tasks which will not resolve the problem. An approaching alliance defines the therapeutic task as all measures necessary to resolve the problem which the family has contracted with the therapist to work on. An avoidant alliance is composed of tasks which are not oriented toward resolving the problem.

The therapist's personal family life experience can either facilitate or impede his/her ability to engage in the appropriate therapeutic tasks. The therapist can assume roles or employ coping mechanisms which are either helpful, benign, or harmful to the goals of the therapeutic contract. The therapist's own developmental stage and current life issues can facilitate his/her ability to pursue the appropriate tasks or they can cloud the therapist's objectivity and lead to the imposition of his/her own unresolved issues upon the family's goals.

System Maintaining or System Changing Alliances

The therapist must establish an alliance that requires the family to deal with the presenting problem in a manner that is somehow different from the ineffective methods they have been using. If the therapist is limited to a narrow range of coping skills, a low degree of differentiation, or a constricted repertoire of emotional expressiveness, then the task dimension of the alliance may not be involving the family in doing anything significantly different. If the therapist allies with the family in a manner that reinforces the family structure which is already maintaining the problem (Feldman & Pinsof, 1982), then the therapist has formed a system maintaining alliance.

If, however, the therapist is able to relate to the family unit in a manner that forces them to relate to him/her in a new way, then the therapist has formed a system changing alliance. Possibly the best example of a therapist's personal presentation making a difference is in Bowen's discussion (1978) of the need for the therapist to maintain a high degree of differentiation in dealing with poorly differentiated families. Bowen emphasizes that the therapist's level of differentiation is a function of his/her personal family life rather than his/her training.

Therapists' personal lives can enrich the therapy when they bring new coping skills or the ability to create a more facilitative emotional atmosphere. They then can form alliances which facilitate system change by utilizing personal abilities that induce client families to engage in new ways of relating and dealing with problems.

Insensitivity or Sensitivity to the Alliance

If therapy is to be effective, establishment of a strong therapeutic alliance is essential. The therapist must recognize that the alliance is forged with the entire patient system, which may include individuals who are not present in the sessions. Family therapists should be cognizant of the interface between the developmental points of the patient family and the therapist's own personal family life. If the therapist ignores important differences between the patient system and his/her own life, then credibility may never develop. The therapist who lacks common experience with the patient system must recognize this fact as a potential threat to the therapeutic alliance and be prepared to deal with it and be able to generalize from other life experiences that create similar feelings and responses. A family may remain in therapy while never making the kind of alliance with the therapist that gives the therapist permission and access to influence them.

Family therapists who are sensitive to the alliance maintain a keen awareness of its multiple interpersonal levels. They bear in mind that their relationship with one individual will impact upon their relationship with another. Further, the therapist's awareness of the family as a system creates an additional level of complexity as the therapist must always attend to his/her alliance with the whole family as well as with the individual members. Therapists who are insensitive to the multiple interpersonal levels of the alliance often sabotage their own efforts by damaging the alliance at one level while appearing to improve it at another. The interpersonal levels of the alliance with families can be viewed hierarchically and the systemic level must receive highest priority, followed by the most powerful subsystems, and then the individual alliances.

IMPLICATIONS FOR TRAINING OF FAMILY THERAPISTS

One conclusion emerging from this paper is that family and marital therapists need to be trained to (1) attend to the therapeutic alliance and, to (2) evaluate and use their personal life experience in developing and maintaining therapeutic alliances with different types of families at different points in treatment. In order to accomplish these goals, we recommend the inclusion of several components in family therapy training programs. The first is a much greater focus on alliance theory. Family and marital therapy trainees need to have a cognitive structure for understanding and attending to the alliance. They need to recognize its existence on different levels and learn to develop techniques for addressing it on each of those levels. They must recognize that different families require different types of alliances and, as therapy progresses, different dimensions of the alliance may need to be emphasized in order to accomplish different therapeutic objectives.

The second training component we recommend is that therapists be required to have training experiences in which they begin to explore the nature of their current and family of origin experiences so they may better understand the influence these key relationships have upon them. Clearly, implementation of this objective would require a sensitive and confidential approach on the part of trainers and fellow trainees. Treatment may be recommended for trainees with major problems stemming from their family lives.

The third element we recommend is that training programs have some mechanism for helping students link the two components presented above. They need to be able to (1) understand the impact of their own family experiences, (2) be knowledgeable about the vicissitudes of the therapeutic alliance, and (3) use their own personal family experiences in establishing and maintaining viable alliances with patient families. This third component is the most difficult, it means helping student therapists to personalize their skills so that they can take greatest advantage of their personal life experiences. It requires trainers to acknowledge that there is no single "right" way to do therapy and focus on helping each student develop their own individual approach, based on their unique strengths and weaknesses.

The task of developing one's unique style as a therapist is often left to the student. Paying greater attention to the interaction between a trainee's personal life experiences and the alliances they form with their patient families is a demanding process. In order for training programs to accomplish this, they must devote considerable time and attention to each trainee. However, the return on this investment would be the development of therapists who are better able to consciously use themselves, not just techniques.

CONCLUSION

The therapeutic alliances formed by family therapists are strongly influenced by their personal family lives. The therapist's personal family life has both immediate and remote determinants and, if unexamined, can play a major (though unconscious) role in shaping the therapist's ideas about fairness, normalcy, and the appropriateness of roles in family life. The therapist cannot escape his/her background but may be able to use it advantageously in building certain kinds of alliances. It is imperative that therapists be aware of the nature of their personal family experiences and the influence these experiences exert upon them.

Family therapists must also be sensitive to the multiple levels of the therapeutic alliance which occur between the therapist system and the patient system. Family therapists establish alliances with systems as well as with individuals and sometimes encounter situations where different levels of the alliance have conflicting goals. It is helpful for the therapist to think about the task, goal, and bond dimensions of the alliance and to examine each of these across the interpersonal levels of the alliance. Finally, therapists can assess the quality of their alliance by considering whether they are: (1) avoiding or approaching the tasks necessary to resolve the problem, (2) forcing the system to change or helping the system maintain its structure, and (3) being sensitive or insensitive to the ongoing maintenance of the multiple levels of the therapeutic alliance.

REFERENCES

Ackerman, N. W. (1966). *Treating the troubled family*. New York: Basic Books.

Aponte, H. J. & VanDeusen, J. M. (1981). Structural family therapy. In A. S. Gurman and D. P. Kniskern (Eds.), *Handbook of family therapy* (pp. 310-360). New York: Brunner/Mazel.

Barrett-Lennard, G. T. (1962). Dimensions of therapist response as causal factors in therapeutic change. *Psychological Monographs, 76*, 1-56.

Bibring, E. (1937). Therapeutic results of psychoanalysis. *International Journal of Psychoanalysis*, *18*, 170-189.

Bordin, E. S. (1979). The generalizability of the psychoanalytic concept of the working alliance. *Psychotherapy: Theory, Research and Practice*, *16*(3), 252-260.

Boszormenyi-Nagy, I. (1965). Intensive family therapy as process. In I. Boszormenyi-Nagy and J. L. Framo (Eds.), *Intensive family therapy: Theoretical and practical aspects* (pp. 87-142). New York: Harper & Row.

Bowen, M. (1961). The family as the unit of study and treatment. *American Journal of Orthopsychiatry*, *31*, 40-60.

Bowen, M. (1978) *Family therapy in clinical practice*. New York: Jason Aronson.

Catherall, D. R. (1984). *The therapeutic alliance in individual, couple, and family therapy*. Ann Arbor: Dissertion Abstracts International.

Catherall, D. R. (1986). The support system and amelioration of PTSD in Vietnam veterans. *Psychotherapy*, *23*(3), 472-482.

Charney, I. W. (1982). The personal and family mental health of family therapists. In F. W. Kaslow (Ed.), *The international book of family therapy* (pp. 41-55). New York: Brunner/Mazel.

Chessick, R. D. (1974). *The technique and practice of intensive psychotherapy*. New York: Jason Aronson.

Cozby, P. W. (1973). Self disclosure: A literature review. *Psychological Bulletin*, *79*, 73-91.

Curtis, C. (1979). The concept of the therapeutic alliance: Implications for the widening scope. *Journal of the American Psychoanalytic Association*, *27*(Suppl.), 159-192.

Davatz, U. (1981). Establishing a therapeutic alliance in family systems therapy. In A. S. Gurman (Ed.), *Questions and answers in the practice of family therapy* (pp. 46-49). New York: Burnner/Mazel.

Dickes, R. L. (1975). Technical considerations of the therapeutic and working alliances. *International Journal of Psychoanalytic Psychotherapy*, *4*, 1-24.

Dryden, W. & Hunt, P. (1985a). Therapeutic alliances in marital therapy: I. Pre-therapy influences. In W. Dryden (Ed.), *Marital therapy in Britain. Volume I: Context and therapeutic approaches*. London: Harper & Row.

Dryden W. & Hunt, P. (1985b). Therapeutic alliances in marital therapy: II. Process issues. In W. Dryden (Ed.), *Marital therapy in Britain. Volume I: Context and therapeutic approaches*. London: Harper & Row.

Feldman, L. B. & Pinsof, W. M. (1982). Problem maintenance in family systems. An integrative model. *Journal of Marital and Family Therapy*, 295-308.

Framo, (1982). *Explorations in marital and family therapy*. New York: Springer.

Frank, J. (1961). *Persuasion and healing*. Baltimore: Johns Hopkins, 1973.

Freud, S. (1912). The dynamics of transference. *The Standard Edition of the complete psychological works of Sigmund Freud*. Vol. 12. London: Hogarth Press, 1958, 97-108.

Gilbert, S. J. (1976). Self disclosure, intimacy and communication in families. *The Family Coordinator*, *25*(3), 221-231.

Greenson, R. R. (1965). The working alliance and the transference neurosis. *Psychoanalytic Quarterly*, *34*, 155-181.

Greenson, R. R. & Wexler, M. (1969). The non-transference relationship in the psychoanalytic situation. *International Journal of Psychoanalysis*, *50*, 27-39.

Gurman, A. S. & Kniskern, D. P. (1978). Research on marital and family therapy: Progress, perspective and prospect. In S. L. Garfield and A. E. Bergin (Eds.), *Handbook of psychotherapy and behavior change: An empirical analysis* (pp. 817-901). New York: John Wiley & Sons.

Gurman, A. S. (1982). Creating a therapeutic alliance in marital therapy. In A. S. Gurman (Ed.), *Questions and answers in the practice of family therapy* Vol. 2 (pp. 15-19). New York: Brunner/Mazel.

Haley, J. (1967). Toward a theory of pathological systems. In G. Zuk & I. Boszormenyi-Nagy (Eds.), *Family therapy and disturbed families*. Palo Alto: Science and Behavioral Books.

Hartmann, H. (1939). *Ego psychology and the problem of adaptation*. New York: International Universities Press, 1958.

Horvath, A. O. & Greenberg, L. S. (1986). The development of the working alliance inventory (WAI). In L. S. Greenberg & W. M. Pinsof (Eds), *The psychotherapeutic process: A research handbook* (pp. 529-556). New York: Guilford Press.

Jackson, D. D. (1957). The question of family homeostasis. *Psychiatric Quarterly Supplement*, *31*, 79-90.

Kanzer, M. (1975). The therapeutic and working alliances. *International Journal of Psychoanalytic Psychotherapy*, *4*, 48-73.

Kaslow, F. W. (1984). Treatment of marital and family therapists. In F. W. Kaslow (Ed.), *Psychotherapy with psychotherapists* (pp. 79-100). New York: Haworth Press.

Kramer, C. H. (1977). Ending family treatment. Paper presented at the 54th Annual Meeting of the American Orthopsychiatric Association, New York.

Kramer, J. R. (1985). *Family interfaces: Transgenerational patterns*. New York: Brunner/Mazel.

Langs, R. (1975). Therapeutic misalliances. *International Journal of Psychoanalytic Psychotherapy*, *4*, 77-105.

Luborsky, L. (1976). Helping alliances in psychotherapy. In *Successful psychotherapy* (pp. 92-116). New York: Brunner/Mazel.

Marziali, E., Marmar, C., & Krupnick, J. (1981). Therapeutic alliance scales: Development and relationship to outcome. *American Journal of Psychiatry*, *138*(3), 361-364.

McGoldrick, M. & Carter, E. A. (1982). The family life cycle. In F. Walsh (Ed.), *Normal family processes* (pp. 167-195). New York: Guilford Press.

Metcoff, J. & Whitaker, C. A. (1982). Family microevents: Communication patterns for problem solving. In F. Walsh (Ed.), *Normal family processes* (pp. 251-276). New York: Guilford Press.

Miller, A. (1981). *Prisoners of childhood*. New York: Basic Books.

Minuchin, S. (1974). *Families and family therapy*. Cambridge: Harvard University Press.

Morgan, R., Luborsky, L., Crits-Cristoph, P., Curtis, H. & Solomon, J. (1982). Predicting the outcomes of psychotherapy by the Penn Helping Alliance Rating Method. *Archives of General Psychiatry*, *39*, 397-402.

Orlinsky, D. E. & Howard, K. I. (1978). The relation of process to outcome in psychotherapy. In S. L. Garfield & A. E. Bergin (Eds.), *Handbook of psychotherapy and behavior change: An empirical analysis* (pp. 283-329). New York: John Wiley & Sons.

Parloff, M., Waskow, I. & Wolfe, B. (1978). Research on therapist variables in relation to process and outcome. In S. L. Garfield & A. E. Bergin (Eds.), *Handbook of psychotherapy and behavior change: An empirical analysis* (pp. 233-282). New York: John Wiley & Sons.

Pinsof, W. M. (1983). Integrative problem-centered therapy: Toward the synthesis of family and individual psychotherapies. *Journal of Marital and Family Therapy*, *9*(1), 19-35.

Pinsof, W. M. (1986). The process of family therapy: The development of the family therapist coding system. In L. S. Greenberg & W. M. Pinsof (Eds.), *The psychotherapeutic process: A research handbook* (pp. 201-284). New York: Guilford Press.

Pinsof, W. M. & Catherall, D. R. (1986). The integrative psychotherapy alliance: Family, couple, and individual therapy scales. *Journal of Marital and Family Therapy*, *12*(2), 137-151.

Rogers, C. R. (1957). The necessary and sufficient conditions of therapeutic personality change. *Journal of Consulting Psychology*, *21*(2), 95-103.

Rutan, S. J. & Smith, J. W. (1985). Building therapeutic relationships with couples. *Psychotherapy*, *22*, 194-200.

Satir, V. (1967). *Conjoint family therapy*. Palo Alto: Science and Behavior Books.

Skynner, A. C. R. (1981). An open-systems, group-analytic approach to family therapy. In A. S. Gurman & D. P. Kniskern (Eds.) *Handbook of family therapy* (pp. 39-84). New York: Brunner/Mazel.

Sluzki, C. (1975). The coalitionary process in initiating family therapy. *Family Process*, *14*, 67-77.

Sprenkle, D. H. & Olson, D. H. L. (1978). Circumplex model of marital systems: An empirical study of clinic and non-clinic couples. *Journal of Marriage and Family Counseling*, April, 59-73.

Sterba, R. (1934). The fate of the ego in analytic therapy. *International Journal of Psychoanalysis*, *15*, 117-126.

Strong, S. R. (1978). Social psychological approach to psychotherapy research. In S. L. Garfield & A. E. Bergin (Eds.), *Handbook of psychotherapy and behavior change: An empirical analysis* (pp. 101-135). New York: John Wiley & Sons.

Strupp, H. H. (1970). Specific vs. nonspecific factors in psychotherapy and the problem of control. *Archives of General Psychiatry*, *23*, 393-401.

Strupp, H. H. (1973). On the basic ingredients of psychotherapy. *Journal of Consulting and Clinical Psychology*, *41*, 1-8.

Strupp, H. H. (1973a). The interpersonal relationship as a vehicle for therapeutic learning. *Journal of Consulting and Clinical Psychology, 41*(1), 13-15.

Strupp, H. H. (1978). The therapist's theoretical orientation: An overrated variable. *Psychotherapy: Theory, Research and Practice, 15*(4), 314-317.

Truax, C. B. (1966). Reinforcement and nonreinforcement in Rogerian psychotherapy. *Journal of Abnormal Psychology, 71*, 1-9.

Vaughn, C. E. & Leff, J. P. (1976). The influence of family and social factors on the course of psychiatric illness: A comparison of schizophrenic and depressed neurotic patients. *British Journal of Psychiatry, 129*, 125-137.

Vaughn, C. E., Snyder, K. S., Jones, S., Freeman, W. R., & Falloon, I. R. H. (1984). Family factors in schizophrenic relapse. *Archives of General Psychiatry, 41*, 1169-1177.

Watzlawick, P., Beavin, J. H., & Jackson, D. D. (1967). *Pragmatics of human communication, A study of interactional patterns, pathologies, and paradoxes*. New York: W. W. Norton & Co.

Zetzel, E. (1956). Current concepts of transference. *International Journal of Psychoanalysis, 37*, 369-376.